The

PRINCIPLE *of*

FATHERHOOD

Priority, Position and the Role of the Male

THE PRINCIPLE OF FATHERHOOD
PRIORITY, POSITION AND THE ROLE OF THE MALE

BY MYLES MUNROE

Copyright © 2000 by Myles Munroe
Printed in the United States of America
ISBN: 1-56229-160-2

Pneuma Life Publishing
4451 Parliament Place
Lanham, MD 20706-1843
1-800-727-3218

Internet: http://www.pneumalife.com

CONTENTS

Dedication

Foreword

Acknowledgements

Preface

Introduction

Chapter One
Fatherhood: The Purpose and Principles *23*

Chapter Two
Father as Source and Progenitor *47*

Chapter Three
Father as Sustainer, Nurturer and Protector *67*

Chapter Four
Father as Teacher *79*

Chapter Five
Father as One Who Disciplines *95*

Chapter Six
Father as Head and Leader *103*

Chapter Seven
Father as One Who Cares *115*

Chapter Eight
Father as Developer *121*

Conclusion

DEDICATION

To all men everywhere, especially in the Third World Nations, who desire to return to the original blueprint of true fatherhood.

To my Dad, my beloved father, the Reverend Matthias E. Munroe, the greatest role model of fatherhood I have in my life—a distinguished man of character, strength, loyalty, commitment, love for my mother, and successful sustainer of eleven grateful and grace-filled children. Thank you, Dad, for living the lessons of life that formed the foundation of the principles in this book.

To my late beloved brother, Paul, who became my twin in life and showed me how to love God without compromise. I know you are now with the Father of fathers.

To my father-in-law, Captain Halton Lockhart, who fathered the woman that has become the wife of my life. Thank you for your steady love and support and for being my other father.

To my beloved son, Chario (Myles) Jr., who makes me live up to the fatherhood image of God. May your sons also become true fathers in their generation.

To my brothers, Oscar and Garth. May you continue to be a model of the Father's love for your wife and children.

To all the members of the Bahamas Faith Ministries Fellowship Real Men Ministry. Thank you for allowing me to teach and develop these principles through your submission to the ministry.

To the born and unborn sons of men who neglected to show them how to be fathers. May this book help father you to become better fathers to your sons.

ACKNOWLEDGEMENTS

Everything we accomplish in life is a synergistic product of many people who have contributed to what we have done and who we have become. This work is no different. I am eternally grateful to all the great men who have inspired, encouraged, and corrected me throughout my development over the years. It takes true fathers to produce true fathers.

I want to thank the following persons for their contribution to the development and completion of this work:

Dad, for laying the foundation for my life so that this book could be not just a theory, but a result of living the principles you taught and lived before me all my life.

For the development and production of this book, I want to thank Mr. Derwin Stewart for his relentless pursuit of me to get this work finished, and the fine editors of Pneuma Life Publishing who labored over this work.

My beloved wife, Ruth, and my precious children, Charisa and Chairo, whose births made me a father and placed demands on me to exemplify the principles of true fatherhood. Thank you for all your patience with me as I developed as a husband and a father.

The many spiritual fathers in my life whose lives and character further refined mine: Dr. Oral Roberts, Dr. Turnel Nelson, Dr. Ezekiel Guti, Reverend Bob Stamps, Reverend Duke Smith, and the late Dr. H.W. Brown.

Finally, to the Father of our Lord Jesus Christ, the Creator and Sustainer of all things, the ultimate Father or fathers, Elohim.

FOREWORD

Being a father is the most fulfilling job a man can have. As Christian parents, we have the unique opportunity to make an eternal investment in the lives of our children.

Jesus often referred to God as "Father". God the Father gives unconditional love, leadership, and guidance. He protects and allows us to learn by His words. God has entrusted us with His sacred title: Father.

In the last few decades, society has strayed away from the importance that fatherhood holds. We have seen the family redefined so much that, in many cases, the father is not even present. The traditional family is fading away, and, with it, we are losing God's blessing and missing the mark.

Becoming a good father is not automatic—it takes time and effort. We must be willing to invest in this job –our most important, second to being a husband– as any other career we might pursue. A father should present the fundamental qualities of leadership, responsibility, and accountability, as well as the capabilities of planning, disciplining, and loving. Fathering is a full-time job. As men, we must train, develop, and learn to be that which God intended for our families.

In his book, *The Principle of Fatherhood*, Dr. Myles Munroe provides a fresh look at time-tested principles for men to measure their effectiveness as fathers in our modern society.

Dr. Munroe teaches how the role, vision, relationship, management, and communication skills of the father within the family structure applies to societies everywhere and at all levels. His fatherhood tips in each chapter challenge me to apply their principles.

In a time when there are classes, books, and workshops for every skill and hobby, I would challenge every father to take time to invest in his most important role–fatherhood. A good father is priceless, as are the children they lead and invest in. We need more good fathers, and this book is an invaluable tool that will indeed help meet that need.

Dr. John C. Maxwell
Author, Speaker, and Founder
The INJOY Group

PREFACE

"Dad is destiny." (*U.S. News and World Report*, Feb. 27, 1995) The words sprang from the page and exploded like an atom bomb. I could not believe what I was reading. Even more surprising was the source from which I was reading those words seemingly taken right from the heart of one of my old seminar sessions. For over twenty years, I have lectured, taught, and counseled thousands of individuals on the subjects of relationships, family development, marriage and effective. One of the greatest concerns I have carried over these living years is the male crisis in which most of our communities find themselves. I have repeatedly stated and emphatically declared that the key to the restoration and preservation of a sane and healthy society is the salvaging of the male, especially as a responsible father. But to read those words on the pages of one of our most popular news magazines was a great cause for encouragement and excitement.

I am a trainer in human and leadership development and serve as Senior Pastor to one of the most dynamic churches in Nassau, Bahamas. Therefore, it was a source of great comfort and relief to see that contemporary behavioral scientists, psychologists, and government bodies were finally agreeing on a conclusion that many of us who deal with social and spiritual matters have known all along.

The statement "Dad is destiny" embodies both the problem and the solution for the majority of society's ills. In it lies the key to the salvation and restoration of mankind. Just over two thousand years ago, the Biblical prophet Malachi spoke of the work and purpose of the coming Messiah by declaring, "He will turn the hearts of the children back to the fathers and the hearts of the fathers back to the children." The implication is that the divine assessment of man's fundamental problem is the fatherless problem.

The *U.S. News and World Report* article stated that more than virtually any other factor, a biological father's presence in the family will determine a child's success and happiness. Without a doubt, this secular article read like a Sunday morning sermon taken from the books of the Bible. It was a refreshing reminder that no matter how far we as a society may stray, it is impossible to effectively ignore, deny, or improve on the ancient wisdom and fundamental truth principles embedded in Biblical records. The Bible establishes in its very first chapter the critical and pivotal role of the male as well as his fatherhood responsibility.

For a brief reality check of our modern-day social status, let us take a short review of life on planet Earth as it relates to the decline of the role and priority of fatherhood and its impact on this and future generations.

Rich or poor, White or Black, the children of divorced parents and those born outside of marriage struggle through life at a measurable disadvantage, according to a growing chorus of social thinkers. By 1996, 28 percent of all children lived without their biological fathers—up from 17.5 percent in 1960. More than half of today's children will spend at least half of their childhood without a father. Many social scientists and behavioral experts agree that external forces like street crime, lousy schools, and economic stress lie behind the crisis in families. In recent studies on social development, it is now a common conclusion that the breakdown in families is what feeds social ills. "Fatherlessness is the most destructive trend of our generation," argues David Blankenhorn, author of the provocative book, *Fatherless America: Confronting Our Most Urgent Social Problem.*

The absence of fathers is linked to most social nightmares—from boys with guns to girls with babies. No welfare reform can cut poverty as thoroughly as a two-parent family. Some 46 percent of children in single-mother families live below the poverty line, compared with 8 percent of those with two parents. Raising marriage rates will do far more to fight crime than building prisons or putting more cops on the streets. Studies show that only 43 percent of state prison inmates grew up with both parents and that a missing father is a better predictor of criminal activity than race or poverty. Having both parents in the home is a better antidote to teen pregnancy than handing out condoms and birth control pills.

Sociologists Sara McLanahan and Gary Sandefur say in their book, *Growing Up With A Single Parent,* that young women who were reared in disrupted families are twice as likely to become teen mothers. Social scientists have made similar links between a father's absence and his child's likelihood of being a school dropout, jobless, a drug addict, a suicide victim, mentally ill, and/or a target of child sexual abuse.

Bringing the issue into sharp focus are some brutal statistical realities. Only 51 percent of kids in most countries still live with both biological parents. At the end of the twentieth century, there were some 1.2 million divorces in the United States alone, about 53 percent of which involved children. In addition, 68 percent of black children and 30 percent of all other children are born outside of marriage. There are places where fathers– usually the best hope to socialize boys–are so rare that bedlam engulfs the community. When it comes to presenting role models to preteen and teenage boys, many teachers, ministers, policemen, and other substitute authority figures often fight losing battles against gang members who are vying to fill the void in those boy's lives. The result is often an astonishing level of violence and incomprehensible incidents of brutality.

In a survey done by *U.S. News and World Report*, 71 percent of those surveyed said, "It is very important for every child to have his or her father living at home," and nearly 8 out of 10 thought that both fathers and mothers should spend more time with their children. Some 58 percent said that it should be harder for couples with children to get a divorce.

It seems simple enough to say that every child needs a father. However, modern experts in the social sciences believe that the greatest positive effects upon a child were shown when the father was a biological, married, and in-residence father. They further argue that the odds are overwhelming against a divorced dad or a father substitute. For proof, they argue that 18 million children in America are entitled to over $34 billion more in child support from non-custodial parents, about 90 percent of whom are fathers. Even the lucky child who sees his or her dad at least once a week–just 1 child in 6–often wind up with a "treat Dad" for weekend movies, not a father that offers constant guidance and discipline.

It even turns out that some fairy tales contain gems of truth about stepparents. Youngsters in stepfamilies do no better, and often fare even worse, than children in homes headed by a single parent, according to several recent studies. Stepparents often bring needed income, but that advantage is often offset by the emotional rivalries among parents and children in stepfamilies.

Finally, the new Traditionalists dispute the idea that children are worse off when stuck in their parents' lousy marriages. "Divorce can increase an adult's happiness, but it is devastating to a child," says psychologist Judith Wallerstein, who has studied her child clients since 1971. One-third report moderate or severe depression five years after a divorce. The hurt may remain hidden for years. Children from divorced families often grow up wary of love, marriage, and family, and over a third have little or no ambition 10 years after their parents part. "Divorce is not just an episode in a child's life," notes Wallerstein. "It's like a natural disaster that really changes the whole trajectory of a child's life."

It would be fair to also point out that we should not generalize and stigmatize absent fathers. Millions try to be good dads, and many children of divorced parents, despite the added risk, seem to turn out fine. Those children are considered the exception rather than the rule. However, research has shown that even those individuals who survived the trauma and negative impact of a broken home or marriage still suffer defects in socio-psychological maladjustments. The emotional, psychological, spiritual, and moral needs met by the loving, caring, balanced environment of a strong marriage and family unit cannot be substituted. It is understandable that there are no perfect human specimens in the human race; however, social sciences have concluded that when an individual is incubated within an atmosphere of love, unity, and caring between two parental elements, there is a definite transfer of those qualities and characteristics to the next generation. In essence, the human family produces after its own kind. The natural logical process of reproduction, which involves the intimate consummation of two individuals, gives evidence that the Creator designed the human family to procreate within the context of a strong, stable union structured to provide the social, psychological, emotional, physical, and spiritual environment for successful development.

There is further evidence to show that there are critical emotional and psychological needs that only a male can provide, just as there are specific needs only the female is designed to meet. Therefore, the absence of either has an effect on development, despite the seemingly normal development and function of the human family.

INTRODUCTION

UNDERSTANDING FATHERHOOD

The greatest enemy of man is ignorance of self. Nothing is more frustrating than not knowing who you are or what to do with what you have. It is debilitating to have something but not know what it is for or how to use it. Even more frustrating is to have an assignment but not know how to do it. Ever had that problem? As a student, did you ever take home a homework assignment and didn't know how to complete it, but you still tried your best to do it all by yourself? Remember that feeling of sitting up all night, trying hard, failing, and, finally, getting angry with everyone, including yourself? How terrible it is to be given something to do but not possess the understanding of how to do it. This is a cause of great distress.

WE LACK UNDERSTANDING

All of mankind's problems are a result of one major dilemma. So, what's this dilemma? Here it is: Possession without understanding; assignment without instruction; resources without knowledge; having everything but not knowing why. Essentially, the dilemma is that we lack understanding. Without understanding, life is an experiment, and frustration is the reward.

I'll never forget bringing home my algebra homework from junior high school in the Bahamas, where I've lived all my life. Ever taken algebra? Remember all of those formulas? For me, it was the most difficult subject in school. Some had an aptitude for math, particularly algebra, geometry or calculus. I didn't. Learning algebra was a horrible experience for me.

Understanding those many formulas was my problem. I remember getting homework assignments consisting of six problems to solve per page. I would go home and just sit there staring at those things. No matter what I did, without understanding the formula, I could not solve the problems.

I would become frustrated to the point of tears. I knew that I would get punished in the morning if I didn't understand the formulas and come up with the correct answers. So, what did I do? I faked it! I wrote down whatever figures came to my mind. Having some numbers written on the page may have looked good, so I thought, but all of the answers were incorrect.

This is more than just an interesting story. You see, when it comes to the issues of life, we often do the same thing I did with my algebra assignments. When problems arise, we fake it. We don't understand the problems, much less life itself, so we fake it. Although I tried to make the figures work out the way I wanted, but I knew they were wrong because I didn't understand the formula. When test time came, my lack of understanding brought me the final result of faking it—failure.

I remember one day I decided I had better learn and understand those formulas, so I took a tutoring course after school with my teacher—just to learn the formulas. It took me hours to learn and understand those formulas, but I put forth the time and effort until I understood. One by one, I began to understand the formulas! Every time I understood them, the lights came on in my mind.

Algebra finally made sense to me and eventually became easy. The fear I had was now replaced with confidence.

After I began understanding algebra, I took my homework assignments home with a smile. Before understanding algebra, I went home with fear. By overcoming my lack of understanding, I then approached those problems with confidence.

The minute you understand and learn the principles of how to do something, then no matter what figures are given to you, you'll just plug them into the proper formula. The figures can change any number of ways, but the formula remains the same. Understanding how to use the formula and how to plug the numbers in correctly gives you the right answer.

Principles are very much like formulas. They are set laws that govern life and are constant in the face of change. So the key, then, is learning and understanding the principles so that you can handle any configuration, any problem, or any situation in life. If you learn to understand the principles of life, then it doesn't matter what life throws at you—just plug the problem into the principle.

The great challenge of life is understanding life. When life throws us a curve ball, we often just play games and fake it. Many times, we have to guess and then wonder endlessly if our guesses will work.

What we lack is understanding. David, the great king of Israel, addressed this very issue. By divine inspiration, he spoke of the moral and social chaos in his community and described the root cause of mankind's confusion, frustration, and self-destruction: *"They know nothing, they understand nothing. They walk about in darkness; all the foundations of the earth are shaken"* (Psalm 82:5).

This text declares that the reason why the earth is so confused and filled with problems is not because there are no answers, but because we don't understand our Creator and we don't know His principles, His purpose, His nature, or His precepts.

THREE THINGS THAT CAUSE PROBLEMS IN LIFE

Psalm 82:5 identifies three progressive components that are the source of our suffering in life. Firstly, there is a lack of knowledge; they know nothing. Secondly, there is a misunderstanding or misconception of life; they understand nothing and cannot comprehend their environment. And thirdly, they walk on in darkness; they see nothing. The word "darkness" as rendered in the Hebrew language context connotes the principle of ignorance. In most cases, its use usually implies the absence of knowledge. Therefore in this context, its use denotes that men are ignorant and blind to God's principles. If you attempt to live and solve the challenges of life from a position of ignorance, then you are walking in darkness and will experience exasperation, frustration, and failure.

The text concludes that ignorance and a lack of understanding result in "all the foundations of the earth are shaken." Foundation implies the fundamental principles and laws that regulate function or operation. In essence, without knowledge and understanding of the basic, fundamental Laws of God, all life goes off track and ends in failure.

When you lack understanding, you will continually use the wrong formula. Knowledge, wisdom and understanding, then, are vital keys to reaching the right answer.

WHAT IS UNDERSTANDING?

Here's a simple definition: Understanding is knowledge and comprehension of the original purpose and intent of a thing. Understanding knows the principles by which a thing was designed to function.

Understanding is 1) the knowledge and comprehension of the original purpose for a thing, and 2) the knowledge of the principles by which the thing was designed to function.

To possess understanding, you must know the original intent for a thing. First, what was in the mind of the one who made it? Second, you must also know how the creator of a product intended that product to function.

Understanding is comprehension of the truth. Now why is this important? Because nothing is truly yours until you understand it. No matter how much you sit and listen, if you don't understand a thing, it's still not yours. You will never truly own or possess a thing that you do not understand. That's why information does not guarantee knowledge. Jesus Christ, the greatest teacher of all time said, "*He who has ears, let him hear*" (Matt. 11:15). He is separating people who simply listen to information from those who actually understand it. When you understand a thing, it becomes yours. Most of our lives are exercises in misunderstanding. We live from the blind side, and for most of us, that encompasses all sides.

Let's take this one step further: Nothing is truly yours until you understand it—including yourself. If you don't understand yourself, you don't possess yourself yet. That is why people who don't know who they are become other people. If you don't know what you were born to be and do, then you become a victim of other people's opinions. Understanding Who made you and who you are is crucial so that others do not take possession of your life. When you understand, then you know what to do with your life.

When I finally learned those algebraic formulas, I then knew what to do with any figure given to me; that principle is so important. You see, once you understand life, then it doesn't matter what life throws at you; you can work out the problem.

In this book, we are going to learn the purpose, principles, and functions of fatherhood so that it doesn't matter what the facts are. You will know, understand, and learn how to recognize the true qualities, character, and function of a true father. Facts will always submit to principle when principle shows up. But if you have facts without principles, facts are going to control and frustrate your life.

Life is only complicated to a man ignorant of principles, for principles are designed to simplify life. Principles protect products. Principles are permanent. Principles preserve. Principles contain inherent judgment. Principles cannot be broken; you break yourself on them. Principles are no respecter of persons. Principles are independent of culture, race, or creed. Principles are the principle thing, and obedience to principles guarantees success.

1

FATHERHOOD: THE PURPOSE AND PRINCIPLES

As I said in my book, *In Pursuit of Purpose*, purpose is inherent in everything that has been created. When a manufacturer creates a new product, the product's intended use and purpose govern the design of that product.

When God created man and woman, he designed them to fulfill their specific function and gave them certain qualities and characteristics to enable them to perform His intended purpose.

God created the male with a particular purpose in mind. He intended for them to be fathers, therefore, He designed them to be so. If men do not know, understand, or fulfill their God-given purpose, then problems will arise both in their identity and relationships.

The inherent purpose within all men is fatherhood.

THE PRINCIPLES OF PURPOSE

Over the past thirty years of studying, counseling, and guiding thousands of individuals to live a life of personal fulfillment and social and spiritual well-being, I have concluded that the key principle of life is purpose. Purpose is the "original intent and reason" for the creation of a thing.

Purpose is the source of all true fulfillment and defines one's existence. Without purpose, life ceases to be an existence, but, instead, becomes an experiment.

As a result of my exploration of this most important issue, I have identified and isolated seven principles of purpose that will assist you in better understanding the nature of life:

1. God is a God of purpose.
2. Everything in life has a purpose.
3. Not every purpose is known.
4. Where purpose is not known, abuse is inevitable.
5. If you want to know the purpose of a thing, never ask the thing.
6. Purpose is only found in the mind of the maker of the thing.
7. Purpose is the key to fulfillment.

FATHERHOOD: THE MALE'S PURPOSE

Equipped with the understanding of the principle of purpose, let us now turn our attention to the concept of the "Fatherhood Principle" and how it relates to the male's purpose.

As noted earlier, everything was created for and to fulfill a purpose in creation and was designed according to the demand of the purpose. Therefore, the unique difference in design that distinguishes each created thing from another is mandated and critical to the purpose and function it is expected to perform. In essence, the difference between the physical, mental, psychological, and dispositional nature of the male and female is providential, essential, valuable, and necessary for the fulfillment of their particular purpose in life. Therefore, the nature of a thing is determined by the purpose of that thing.

The way you are is a result of why you are.

Understanding the purpose for the male is critical and necessary in any attempt to understand "fatherhood", because the male was designated (design-ated) a father by the Creator. This fatherhood is not a choice for a male, but inherent in his nature. Every male is a father by nature. His personal fulfillment is linked to fulfilling that purpose. Though all males were created to be fathers, this must not be confused with the biological production of children, which we will discuss later.

From the Manufacturer's Manual (the Bible), I want to give you the purpose and principles of fatherhood. First, the purpose: The essence of the male man is fatherhood. God had fatherhood in mind when He made the male. He was thinking "father" when He created the male man.

God intends every boy to grow up into fatherhood. As a matter of fact, buried in every boy is a father. I am not just talking about the biological ability the man has within himself to father offspring. Being a "father" is rooted in God's image, because God is Father. He is not satisfied until the father comes out of the boy. Therefore, man must understand fatherhood, or he will never fulfill himself. Fatherhood is the design and destiny of the male.

"FATHER" DEFINED: WHAT IS FATHER?

One of the greatest dangers to society is the misconception of what fatherhood is. Definitions determine interpretations, thus we must begin here. Question: What is father? There are two words used in the Bible that are translated "father." One is in the Old Testament, and it's the Hebrew word "Ab". Two Hebrew consonants spell "father"–aleph and beth. "Abba", meaning Daddy, comes from the root Hebrew word for father, Ab. In the New Testament, the word for father is "pater". So, you have Ab and Abba in Old Testament Hebrew and pater in New Testament Greek.

Now, what does Ab and pater mean? Both words denote very basic concepts, which include the following:

- Source
- Nourisher
- Sustainer
- Supporter
- Founder
- Protector

Therefore, the source and sustainer of a thing is called "Ab," father. As the source, the Ab sustains and maintains. Another part of the meaning of the word "Ab" is upholder. "Father" is the source that upholds everything that comes from it.

Now, there are some other English words related to the words "Ab" and "pater" that describe fatherhood and are absolutely essential to the purpose of a father.

Don't ignore the following words; they are pregnant with meaning:

- *Progenitor*. Remove the prefix from this word and you have "genitor." This is the root word for "generation." Pro-genitor. "Pro" means to support or uphold before, and "genitor" means to generate, or to start. To generate something means that you're the initiator or source of it, and pro means to support and uphold. Therefore, "father" is the source that generates, initiates, and supports that which he generates.

---

*A father is the source that generates generations.
That's why he's called a progenitor.*

Generations come from the Ab and pater–the father–not from the mother. God created man to be father–the progenitor, source, and supporter of generations. The Ab generates everything. That's why there is no seed in women.

- *Ancestor*. Ab and pater also mean ancestor. Ancestor and ancestry ultimately come from the same Latin verb "antecedere", meaning to go before or precede. At the start of an ancestral line is the father. He begins the heritage for all of his seed. This is very important. The man (the father) was given the responsibility not only to start and provide the future generation, but also to give that generation an identity.

For example, when you are born into a normal family relationship, you take your father's name, not your mother's name. That is correct. That's why the women who are trying to use both their maiden and married names should be careful because the divine plan of God is being tampered with. This is very important. When you begin to use your two names, you are attempting to claim and produce two generations and two identities instead of one. This is a source and cause of much confusion in the offspring. In Scripture, there is no such thing as the son of two fathers. God always speaks of lineage to one man—the father.

James, the son of Zebedee, was Zebedee's son, not the son of Zebedee's wife's daddy. Now why is that important? Because the minute you start bringing in another ancestry or lineage, you literally split the fatherhood. There can only be one source. That is why the Bible says, *"For this reason a man will leave his father and mother . . ."* (Matt 19:5). It never says the woman leaves because whenever she marries, she inherits another father.

Hard to understand? Then consider this very carefully: The wife doesn't carry her husband's father's name. She picks up whatever the husband is called, because she picks up another father. Why? All men are fathers. It's tough being a man, because whoever you marry becomes your "child" so to speak. That's what God intended, and that's why wives take on their husband's name. The male man (the father) becomes responsible for his wife one hundred percent. The husband (also the father) provides, sustains, nourishes, upholds, and supports. Even Jesus is never referred to as the "Son of Mary" in Scripture, but rather the "Son of God". *"The Holy Spirit will come upon you, and the power of the Most High will overshadow you. So the holy one to be born will be called the Son of God."* (Luke 1:35)

I know that Jesus was single, but He understood the principle of marriage as explained in Matthew 19. That's why when the disciples understood this from Jesus, they said it was better to stay single (see Matthew 19:10). Jesus said, "You're right." When you take on a woman as your wife, you are not taking on some sex object. You are not taking on someone to brag about, saying, "That's my woman." No, that's your baby! Essentially, your wife is "your baby". Even Jesus, referring to His bride, the church, gave her His name and she is called "the body of Christ." He stressed, "In My name you will ask the Father everything."

Some men wonder why their wives suddenly call them "daddy." A wife may call her husband "daddy" because that is a natural instinct, inherent in the nature of a woman. We have too many husbands who are not "daddies". They are not the Ab or pater that God calls men to be to their wives.

- *Founder.* "Father" also implies founder or foundation. That's why they use "father" as a description in organizations and in different institutions. If someone founded something, they say he's the father of that organization. Why? He generated it. He's the founder that caused the genesis of it. God built the male to found future generations and to be the foundation on which they develop. It is essential to note that the quality of the foundation determines the value of the building. The men who established the constitution of the United States of America are referred to as the "Founding Fathers". Nelson Mandela is known as the "Father of the New

South Africa".

- *Author.* "Father," the Ab, also implies authorship. The triune God in Christ Jesus is the Author of salvation (Hebrews 5:9) and the Author and Finisher of our faith (Hebrews 12:2). "The Author of salvation", what does that mean? Jesus initiated, generated, produced, upholds, and sustains the salvation of all mankind. He is the sole Source of our redemption.

He is the image of the invisible God, the firstborn over all creation. For by him all things were created: things in heaven and on earth, visible and invisible, whether thrones or powers or rulers or authorities; all things were created by him and for him.

(Colossians 1:15-16)

"Author" also denotes the authorized authority of a thing. Therefore, "father" possesses inherent authority. Author means source.

Jesus is the Source of salvation. If you want to come to God, Jesus is the ultimate Source. That's why despite the great works of Mohammed, Buddha, Confucius, or Mr. Moon, according to Scripture, you can't go to either of those men for salvation, because they didn't generate, create, or author man's redemption. Jesus is the Generator of salvation; it germinated with Him. The Scriptures refer to Jesus as the "Author and Finisher" of our faith.

I'm so glad that He's not just the Author. A lot of men are merely authors of babies, but they don't finish as fathers. Jesus is a good Daddy. He's the Finisher of your faith. He didn't just start your faith; He'll see it to the end until it gets finished. He will grow you up to the full stature and measure of His purpose for you so that you look just like Him. (See 2 Corinthians 3:18.) He provides the "gene" for the new generation of man. He is the Source of seed for salvation. All fathers provide the "gene-seed" which determines the quality of the generation he produces. You will note that in Isaiah's description of the Messiah, he concludes with the titles: Wonderful Counselor, Mighty God, EVERLASTING FATHER, Prince of Peace. How did the Son become Father? He generated a new generation of man. He became the "Last Adam" who produced "the Second Man."

- *Teacher.* Ab is the one who teaches and nourishes. This means "father" is one who provides nutrients and resources that develop, enrich, expand, grow, and deploy that which comes from it. One of man's major responsibilities is to teach his "offspring." Many men are found lacking in this area of teaching and are intimidated by the women they marry. Let me say something to men: By nature, the male is wired to teach, so you don't need to know much about teaching techniques. Males, by nature, love to give instruction. The father-instinct of teaching is inherent within men, and it also causes men to resist the attempts women make to instruct them. Father, you're a teacher. Get some knowledge and understanding in order to teach.

For the LORD gives wisdom, and from his mouth come knowledge and understanding. (Proverbs 2:6)

Blessed is the man who finds wisdom, the man who gains understanding, (Proverbs 3:13)

Get wisdom, get understanding; do not forget my words or swerve from them. (Proverbs 4:5)

Fathers, you must get knowledge and understanding from the Word of God so that you can lead your family with wisdom, knowledge, integrity, and confidence. Some men are so ignorant that when they come into the presence of a well-educated woman they are intimidated and feel threatened.

Father, be the Ab. Get smart by getting knowledge, understanding, and wisdom from God.

- *Creator.* Ab also denotes creator. "Father" is one who founds or creates something. The pater becomes the father of it. For example, Thomas Edison, the creator of the light bulb, became the "Father of the light bulb". We often refer to people who created things as the father of it.

In Matthew 6:9, Jesus teaches us to pray, "Our Father, which art in heaven, hallowed be thy name." Isaiah 63:16 declares, *"But you are our Father, though Abraham does not know us or Israel acknowledge us; you, O LORD, are our Father, our Redeemer from of old is your name."* When we use the term "Our Father," we must remember this is not a name but a title resulting from a function. In fact, God was not always a Father, but became "Father" after His creative work. God is called Father because He is the "Source and Sustainer" of everything He created, which makes Him the Father of all things. This is why He is called the Father of creation. Have you ever noticed that God never chose to call Himself "Mother"? Why? Because everything came from Him, but He came from nothing. In truth, the word "god" literally means self-sustaining, self-sufficient one. God is life and gives everything life.

The American feminist movement says, "We've got to change the Bible. The Bible is male chauvinistic because it only refers to God as 'Him' and 'He' and 'Father'". To remedy that, they've written some Bibles which adjust the Scriptures so that it will have more inclusive language. Instead of "Father", God is called "Our Divine One." When they read a Scripture now, instead of saying "him" or "her," they say "person." For example, Jude 24 would read, "Now unto the Person who is able to keep us from falling." Isn't that amazing? They say, "The Lord is my Shepherdess." No wonder they are still found wanting.

What they and too many others don't understand is God's very nature; His very essence is "Father." Why? He's the Source of creation; so, it comes with just being pregnant with the seed. If you produce the seed, you are the father. So "Father" is not just something bestowed upon Him; it's the natural result of Him creating everything.

Jesus and the Father are one. We saw in Isaiah 63:16 that even if Abraham doesn't take responsibility to be our father, God is still our Father. All of us came out of God, the Father. Take note once again of the powerful revelation given about Jesus:

For to us a child is born, to us a son is given, and the government will be on his shoulders. And he will be called Wonderful Counselor, Mighty God, Everlasting Father, Prince of Peace. (Isa. 9:6)

How is it that the child went from being the Son to being the Father? Easy, because the Father is the Son. When He–the Son–showed up on Earth, He came out of the Father, but They are one. The Father and the Son are one! (See John 10:30.) In John 1:1, we read, *"In the beginning was the Word, and the Word was with God, and the Word was God."* So whatever part of God came out of God, that is called Son, but it's still Father because it is God. So for His atonement purposes, He's Son, but when it comes to responsibility, He's Father.

Here's an example: When the Jews started to talk to Jesus about Abraham, they said, "We know who our father is." They tried to put Jesus down by saying He didn't know who His Father was. They told Jesus, "You're a bastard. You were born out of wedlock. You don't know who your daddy is. We know who our father is; our father is Abraham" (see John 8). Jesus said, "Don't you know that before Abraham was, I am. In other words, Abraham came out of Me; I am Abraham's Father." It's tough to tell God anything about being a daddy; afterall, He is Abba–the Source of all created things.

James 1:17 reveals that God is "the Father of lights." That means stars, suns, moons and everything that exists in the universe came out of God. All creation came out of God. God is the Father of all that exists. That's why Ephesians 1:17 declares, "He is the Father and God of our Lord Jesus Christ." Why? The Son came from the Father. So He's the Creator of all things, therefore, He's Father. The source, the essence, the very being of the Father is the Son.

The early Christians understood this. At the Council of Nicea (325 A. D.) they wrote in the Nicean Creed: [Bold is my emphasis.]

"We believe in one God, the **Father** almighty, maker of all things, visible and invisible; And in one Lord Jesus Christ, the Son of God, begotten from the Father, only-**begotten, that is from the substance of the Father**, God from God, light from light, true God from true God, *begotten not made, of one substance with the Father*, through whom all things came into being, things in heaven and things on earth . . ." (Quoted from Urban, Linwood. *A Short History of Christian Thought*, p. 64. New York: Oxford University Press, 1995).

Hebrews 12:9 reveals that God is "*the Father of spirits.*" All spirits came out of Him. Why? He is Spirit (John 4:24). Whatever God creates came out of Him. Whether it is material or spirit, God is still the Father of it. He made Himself Father by virtue of His creative will. He is the Source of all spirits because He created them all.

Acts 17:26 reads, "*From one man He made every nation of men, that they should inhabit the whole earth . . .*" From God's own image came the male man (Genesis 1:27), and from that man (Adam) came all humanity. That is why when you look at the genealogy of Adam, it concludes with the term, "Adam who was the son of God." In essence, whoever the source is, that's also the Abba, the father.

Which was the son of Enosh, the son of Seth, the son of Adam, the son of God. (Luke 3:38)

You cannot be a father unless you are willing to uphold that which comes out of you.

There is a catch here. God only refers to Himself as Father. God sustains all things that came out of Him. God the Father made all the worlds through the Son and upholds all things by the power of His Word.

> *But in these last days he has spoken to us by his Son, whom he appointed heir of all things, and through whom he made the universe. The Son is the radiance of God's glory and the exact representation of his being, sustaining all things by his powerful word. After he had provided purification for sins, he sat down at the right hand of the Majesty in heaven.*
> *(Heb. 1:2-3)*

God upholds everything by the power of His Word. Therefore, whatever God produced, He upholds. God the Father is the perfect Model, Example, and Mentor for all men who desire to be true fathers.

THE PRINCIPLES OF FATHERHOOD

We all understand that a principle is a fundamental law that governs function and behavior. Therefore, we must understand the basic laws of fatherhood in order to be effective fathers. The father (Ab and pater) is the source that sustains, protects, nourishes, and provides identity for that which he produces.

You are a father of someone when you are: the source, the sustainer, the protector, the provider, the nourisher, the progenitor, and the identity.

Do you know what's the greatest challenge for our young men today? They suffer from an identity crisis. Why? Because they lacked the nurturing influence of a true father to give them identity. An identity doesn't come from a gang or the government or books. Identity comes from a father.

There's something about a male man that's very interesting. A man needs to be affirmed by a father in order to confirm his manhood. The only one who can make you understand your manhood is a father. Most young men are running around looking for a father, but they can't find him. They're running to their brothers, but to no avail. You can't find fatherhood in another peer who is also looking for a father. You cannot discover who you are by looking to someone who doesn't know who he or she is. You've got to get your identity from a father. That's why many young men yearn for years just to hear their fathers say to them, "I love you, son. You're a man now."

The only one who can give a man his identity as a man is a father. This fundamental principle is lacking in many of our cultures, and its absence is the source of many social problems.

Do you know why being Jewish carries with it such a strong identity? Jewish tradition, particularly in family relationships within their genealogy, has a very real sense of the "father" spirit. This is rooted in a ceremony called "bar mitzvah", in which a twelve-year old Jewish boy goes before the men and performs some prescribed traditional rites, after which the men say to him, "Now thou art a man." From that day forward, that boy takes on a different spirit, for he is now a man. That's why their communities are knitted so closely together and they're so strong in business, tradition, and culture.

Jewish fathers tell and show their boys what it means to have the identity of a man. This cultural practice is embedded in their history and can be traced back to Biblical roots. This practice can also be found in many African and Eastern cultures where manhood is bestowed through a ritual.

Now pay close attention: If you haven't found your father yet, *God* qualifies as your Father. Hallelujah! You can come to God and say, "God, what am I?" and He'll tell you, "You're My son." That's the first thing He'll tell you. Brother, get your identity from Him.

> *Yet to all who received him, to those who believed in his name, he gave the right to become children of God.*
> *(John 1:12)*

Secondly, God the Father will say to you, "Now mature into the image of My dear Son, Jesus Christ, and you will grow up in Him until you are a true man." Jesus, who is Father, tells you "thou art a father." He gives you your identity as a father.

The principle of fatherhood is simple: You provide identity. God created man to be the father of the family. Once again, God created the male man to be the father of mankind's family. That's why He made the male first.

May I take that a little further? God created one human being from the soil and never went back to the soil to create another human being. God placed all men in that first male; this is a mystery. He went to the soil once (Genesis 2:7) and never went back again. In the creation record in the Book of Genesis, God made only one man from the soil—one person, one body. God never went back to the soil. Everything God wanted for the human race was in that one man. God went to the soil, carved out one male, stood him up, breathed life into him, created out of that man a woman, and then God said, "*Now be fruitful*" (Gen. 1:28).

In that one man (Adam) was every other male and female in history. Why? Because God wanted the man– the male man–to be the father and the source. He designed him to be the father. That's why He didn't go back to the soil. The male man is father, not by vote or cultural positioning, but by virtue of his disposition in the process of creation.

Every male man is created with the responsibility of fatherhood, because God designed the male to be the source. That's why every male carries with him right now millions of sperm, because he is the "source". Men have been prepared by God to be fathers.

God took everybody, put them in one body, and made that one body the source of everybody.

God placed all men in the male man (Adam), and God only created one man from the soil. The Creator made the male man the source of all men. Why? Because he–the Ab and pater–was to represent God.

Just as God is the Father of all living things, He made man to be the father of the human family. Therefore, the male was created, designed, and designated by virtue of his nature and purpose to be a "father".

Every man, whether married or not, has an inherent identity and purpose to be a "father". You're destined to be a father by the simple fact that you're a male. Therefore, fatherhood is not necessarily having a baby; fatherhood is simply being a male. If you are a male, then you are responsible for anything that comes out of you. The female came out of you, and you are responsible for anything that comes out of the female who came out of you! Paul refers to this principle and responsibility of the male as the principle source of the human family:

> *Now I want you to realize that the head of every man is Christ, and the head of the woman is man, and the head of Christ is God . . . For man did not come from woman, but woman from man . . . In the Lord, however, woman is not independent of man, nor is man independent of woman. (1 Cor. 11:3,8,11)*

The male man is distinguished by the following principles:

- *The male is the source of seed.* The male is the host of the sperm (genes that provide the genetic pool for the generations to come). He is the source of "human life", whereas the woman is the incubator of life. It is the woman that gives life to the man's seed.

- *The male is the nourisher of fruit.* Seed comes out, gets planted, and then becomes a tree. A tree bears fruit. Whatever comes out of the seed is fruit, so therefore you, father, are responsible for nourishing the fruit. The seed supplies the tree that sustains the fruit that, in turn, produces more seed. Father means nourisher.

- *The male is the source of females.* First Corinthians 11:8 says, *"For man did not come from woman, but woman from man."* Therefore, the glory of the man is the woman. In other words, the man is responsible for what came out of him. Every woman is man's offspring. So if you are dating a young girl, you are, in essence, dating your "daughter". Any man that rapes a woman is also raping his "daughter" and committing incest. That's why when Solomon referred to his lover, he said, *"How delightful is your love, my sister, my bride!"* (Song of Solomon 4:10). A woman is your sister first–family, offspring–then she becomes your bride. You are never to lay with her until she becomes your bride. When a woman goes out with a man, she's supposed to feel protected, because, theoretically, she's out with her "father". So when you hold hands with your girlfriend, remember, you're holding hands with your sister, your daughter, or your family; therefore, make sure it's a holy and fatherly holding of hands. When you kiss her, be certain it's a fatherly kiss. That's why she's supposed to feel safe with you at 2:00 in the morning when all the lights are off by the beach and near the coconut tree. She's with her "father".

Jesus, who is our Husband–our Bridegroom–is also our Father. Jesus and the Father are one. He provides. He protects. He nourishes. He supplies. He gives and doesn't abuse.

Can you imagine slapping your wife (daughter)? A lot of men kick, slap, and curse their wife (daughter), and think they're real men. They are not real men; they are imposters and fools ignorant of their God-given purpose. Such ignorant men are dangerous because where purpose is not known, abuse is inevitable. Remember, whatever comes out of you is a part of you. If a man hates his wife, the he also hates himself. That's why the Bible says, "*After all, no one ever hated his own body*" (Eph. 5:29). Why? That's your baby, which came from you. If a man loves his wife, he loves his own flesh, the Bible says. That's why the Word says, "*Love your wife as yourself.*" (See Eph. 5:25-31.) A man that walks around slapping, kicking, and cursing himself is called a crazy man. The principle is this: The male is the source of the female. She is your offspring. Father means source!

- *The male is designed to protect his fruit.* That's the reason for your strength, men. God gave the male physical strength and physique. His bone structure is heavier and bigger than the woman's, not to beat her, but to protect her. The safest place for a woman should be in the arms of her husband, her Abba. If she can't be safe there, she's in trouble. Fatherhood is an awesome responsibility, because you then become the progenitor of all that comes out of you and must protect all that comes out of you. Father means protector.

- *The male determines the type and quality of the offspring.* Because you carry the seed within you, you also carry the type of tree it will become . So I say this to all women: Be careful about the type of seed you receive in your soil. There are some thorns and some bad seeds. Some men are walking around that *look* like good fruit, but they're really gooseberries.

Remember, the male determines the quality and the type of seed. So when women think about marriage, they should make sure they understand the nature, quality, and type of seed that is within the man they want to marry. Whatever you receive, you will produce. Whatever you sow, you will reap. (See Galatians 6:7.) The male carries the seed.

Men, you must also be careful about what kind of soil you plant your seed into. The seed may be good, but if the soil has poor nutrition in it, then you will have a sick tree. Good seed should never be just strewn about anywhere. You want quality soil for your seed in order to guarantee good trees. The quality of the woman affects the quality of the fruit. Father means quality management.

- *The male maintains his offspring.* The father principle is to maintain. The male is responsible for the security, sustenance, and development of his seed. Father means maintenance.

- *The male teaches his seed.* He gives his seed knowledge. A male is a godly father when he takes responsibility for his seed. The source must sustain, train, and instruct the resource. That is fatherhood. Most women are doing the teaching and the training, but God says that fathers are to do the teaching and training in the home. That means that you as the male man are responsible not only for having babies, but also for training those babies and teaching them so that they can walk in the way of the Lord.

*It's difficult to lead children to the Lord if
you are an absentee father. It's hard to take people to
where God is if you are not heading that way
yourself. You cannot lead your family to
where you are not going.*

THE FUNCTIONS OF FATHERHOOD

Are you ready to become the father that the Father created you to be? Do you know what a father is to do? Do you know how a father should talk and act? Well, the standard by which we should measure and train fathers can be found within these ten basic functions of true fatherhood:

1. Progenitor
2. Source
3. Sustainer & Nourisher
4. Protector
5. Teacher
6. Disciplinarian
7. Leader
8. Head
9. Caring One
10. Developer

My brother, you can be the father God has purposed you to be. The coming chapters will teach you God's functions inherent in your purpose as a "father"–Ab and pater. Let us move on to fatherhood.

Principles

- Fatherhood is not a choice for a male, but inherent in his very nature. His personal fulfillment will always be linked to fulfilling that God-given purpose.

- You cannot be a father unless you are willing to uphold that which comes out of you. "Father" means the source that sustains—the true role and purpose of the male man.

- The only one who can give a man his identity as a man is a father (Ab or pater).

- God designed the man to be the source. He took everybody, put them in one body, and made that one body the source of everybody.

- The ten functions of fatherhood are:
  1. Progenitor
  2. Source
  3. Sustainer & Nourisher
  4. Protector
  5. Teacher
  6. Disciplinarian
  7. Leader
  8. Head
  9. Caring One
  10. Developer

2

FATHER AS SOURCE AND PROGENITOR

The highest honor that God can give the male man is to designate him a father. That does not mean that he is bigger or stronger than the female. "Father" is the title or designation that God chose for Himself. God does not call Himself "Mother". So if God chooses "Father" as His own title and conveys it upon the man, then it must be the highest title, designation, and honor that any human being can have. In fact, fatherhood is the ultimate work of the male man. Fatherhood is a heavy honor and tremendous responsibility.

A male can do nothing greater than fathering. He can earn a million dollars, but if he fails to fulfill God's calling upon him to father as God fathers, then he is a failure. He can own a huge home, have tremendous real estate holdings, manage a large stock portfolio, and have a billion-dollar estate, but if he fails to father his family and children, he's a failure.

A man that is physically strong but weak as a father is not a man. A man rich in possessions but poor in fathering is not a man. A man eloquent in words but silent as a father in teaching his household the Word and precepts of God is not a father. Thus, the measure of a man's success is directly related to his effectiveness as a godly father, for which God is the only true example and standard.

THE SOURCE OF SIN IS FATHERLESSNESS

At the root of sin is the absence of real fathers in our world. The sin problem is a fatherhood problem, because sin is the result of a man–Adam–declaring independence from God, his Source and Father. Adam believed he didn't need a father and that he could be a father without the Father. That is when the human race fell into rebellion against God.

Sin is the result of a man–Adam–turning his back on his Father.

One of the root meanings of the word sin (armatia) is separation. Adam separated himself from his Father and thus fell into a state of separation and sin. In other words, man could be called a "fatherless child" because of his own choice. Imagine that. Orphaned by choice! Homeless by choice! Separated from his Father by choice! How tragic was the choice of Adam to reject his Father!

Salvation is the result of a man–Jesus, the Second Adam–providing us with the way to return to the Father. When the Second Adam, Jesus, came to earth, He returned the orphaned children of humanity back to their Father, God. Remember, Adam left his Father. The mission of Jesus was to return humanity–fatherless, orphaned humanity–back to the Father. Malachi prophesied that this would happen when John the Baptist prepared the way for the Messiah: *"He will turn the hearts of the fathers to their children, and the hearts of the children to their fathers; or else I will come and strike the land with a curse"* (Mal. 4:6).

Adam was a fatherless child, and Adam had children. The first child that came out of Adam was a female–Eve. Adam's first baby was not Cain; Adam's first baby was a woman named Eve. Every child after Eve was fatherless because there was no God-Father. Since Adam was fatherless, all of his descendents were also fatherless, starting with Eve.

God breathed life into Adam. *"The LORD God formed the man from the dust of the ground and breathed into his nostrils the breath of life, and the man became a living being"* (Gen. 2:7). But, Adam cut himself off from God, his Father–the Source of his creation and life. Once Adam became fatherless, all he could pass on to his children was death.

The father can only create or generate in his children what he has received from his father. Father is the source, the creator, the generator, and the progenitor. Future generations can only receive what the father gives them.

Since Adam rejected his Father, thereby rendering himself fatherless, the only inheritance he had to give to future generations was sin and death–a fatherless inheritance. As a fatherless child, Adam's bequest to humanity was fatherlessness.

One more point needs to be made here before I discuss Malachi 4:6 in depth. If Adam's first child was a woman, and Adam was fatherless, then all women, starting with Eve, are fatherless. That means women are looking for just one thing–a father, not a husband. They are suffering from fatherlessness. All too often, women are lost and making so many mistakes because all they have in the house is a husband, not a father. What they need is a father who can teach them about the Father, God.

Without fathers, there is a curse upon women and future generations. In essence, every husband must also become his wife's father.

TURNING THE HEART OF THE CHILDREN TO THEIR FATHERS

John the Baptist came preparing the way for Jesus. Through Jesus, the heart of the children would be turned back to their fathers. Jesus came to fix man's problem of fatherlessness. Many fathers are estranged from their children. Many homes are fatherless. Before Christ, Adam's children throughout the ages knew nothing about the Father because they started fatherless as a result of Adam's sin and rejection of God the Father. The problem of being fatherless started with Adam and still affects us to this day.

Brothers, our nations could be healed right now if every man became a responsible father. The ten functions of fatherhood outlined in the previous chapter will certainly help point us back to God the Father. We have already seen the first two functions of fatherhood in Genesis. God, our Father, is both our Progenitor and Source. Jesus, God's Son, showed us the way back to the Father. Returning us to our Progenitor and Source was Jesus' mission. Humanity needed to return to God the Father.

Luke 1:16-17 described the setting into which Jesus the Messiah would come: "*Many of the people of Israel will he [Elijah] bring back to the Lord their God. And he will go on before the Lord, in the spirit and power of Elijah, to turn the hearts of the fathers to their children and the disobedient to the wisdom of the righteous—to make ready a people prepared for the Lord.*" The people needed to return to God the Father. John the Baptist was preparing them for what they desperately needed–One who could lead them back to the Father.

A family or nation is not in order until the father is back in his position. Until men are restored to their position of fathering like the Father, the people cannot be healed.

Men and women alike are looking for a father. Without the Father, a husband does not know how to father his wife or children. Without a father in the home, women end up babysitting their husbands. They take care of the man who is supposed to father them.

Jesus knew the Father and became the Progenitor and Source of a new race of fathers–the children of God who knew their heavenly Father through Jesus, the Father's Son. You cannot be a true father unless you have one. The only person in history who could father us was One who had known the Father, and that person was Jesus.

For example, Jesus was dying on the cross, but He took the time as well as a few of his last fleeting breaths to father His mother. He gave instructions as the head, the oldest son left in His family. Some have concluded that at the time of Jesus' crucifixion, Joseph was dead, thereby leaving Jesus as the father of the home. *"When Jesus saw his mother there, and the disciple whom he loved standing nearby, he said to his mother, "Dear woman, here is your son," and to the disciple, "Here is your mother"* (John 19:26-27). Jesus fulfilled the responsibilities of fathering in His house because His earthly father had died. In those statements, Jesus put the responsibility of caring for his mother, Mary, in John's hands.

If you are the son in a home where your daddy has left, then you are the father of your mother, your sisters, and your household. Why? Because God has called men to be fathers like Him in order to turn the heart of the children back to the Father, God. If you understand this principle and responsibility and begin to apply it in your life, then God will answer your prayers for provision, because He will father you as you also father your family.

JESUS AND HIS FATHER

The greatest example of the critical role of father was demonstrated in the life of Jesus Christ Himself. He spoke of His Father more than anyone else. He expressed and emphatically confessed His need, dependency, and submission to His Father at every opportunity. He never hesitated to give credit to His Father for any activity or success in His life, thereby confirming the sustaining work of God in His life. He saw His Father as the Source, Resource, Cause, and Purpose for His entire life.

Whenever He was questioned about His identity, His work, His purpose, His heritage, His power, His authority, His family, His message, His philosophy, His theology, His legitimacy or His destiny, He referred to "My Father."

How many men do you know today that speak of their father in such a way? How many could and do give their father credit for most of their activities and success-es? On the contrary, most men today consider it "less manly" to refer to or give credit to another because it is perceived as a weakness. What a stark contrast to the attitude of the Ultimate Man, Jesus Christ! His perception and relationship with His Father should serve as the standard by which we measure the effectiveness and success of true fatherhood. In essence, the level at which your child refers to you is the measure of your effectiveness as a father.

Then they asked him, "Where is your father?" "You do not know me or my Father," Jesus replied. "If you knew me, you would know my Father also."
(John 8:19)

"I have much to say in judgment of you. But he who sent me is reliable, and what I have heard from him I tell the world." They did not understand that he was telling them about his Father. So Jesus said, "When you have lifted up the Son of Man, then you will know that I am the one I claim to be and that I do nothing on my own but speak just what the Father has taught me. The one who sent me is with me; he has not left me alone, for I always do what pleases him."
(John 8:26-29)

I am telling you what I have seen in the Father's presence, and you do what you have heard from your father. (John 8:38)

"I am not possessed by a demon," said Jesus, "but I honor my Father and you dishonor me." (John 8:49)

Jesus replied, "If I glorify myself, my glory means nothing. My Father, whom you claim as your God, is the one who glorifies me. Though you do not know him, I know him. If I said I did not, I would be a liar like you, but I do know him and keep his word."
(John 8:54-55)

Jesus answered, "I did tell you, but you do not believe. The miracles I do in my Father's name speak for me." (John 10:25)

My Father, who has given them to me, is greater than all; no one can snatch them out of my Father's hand. I and the Father are one. (John 10:29-30)

Do not believe me unless I do what my Father does. But if I do it, even though you do not believe me, believe the miracles, that you may know and understand that the Father is in me, and I in the Father. (John 10:37-38)

Jesus knew that the Father had put all things under his power, and that he had come from God and was returning to God. (John 13:3)

Philip said, "Lord, show us the Father and that will be enough for us." Jesus answered: "Don't you know me, Philip, even after I have been among you such a long time? Anyone who has seen me has seen the Father. How can you say, 'Show us the Father'? Don't you believe that I am in the Father, and that the Father is in me? The words I say to you are not just my own. Rather, it is the Father, living in me, who is doing his work. Believe me when I say that I am in the Father and the Father is in me; or at least believe on the evidence of the miracles themselves." (John 14:8-11)

On that day you will realize that I am in my Father, and you are in me, and I am in you. Whoever has my commands and obeys them, he is the one who loves me. He who loves me will be loved by my Father, and

I too will love him and show myself to him.
(John 14:20-21)

I am the true vine, and my Father is the gardener.
(John 15:1)

This is to my Father's glory, that you bear much fruit,
showing yourselves to be my disciples. "As the Father
has loved me, so have I loved you. Now remain in my
love. If you obey my commands, you will remain in
my love, just as I have obeyed my Father's commands
and remain in his love." (John 15:8-10)

I no longer call you servants, because a servant does
not know his master's business. Instead, I have called
you friends, for everything that I learned from my
Father I have made known to you. (John 15:15)

Though I have been speaking figuratively, a time is
coming when I will no longer use this kind of language
but will tell you plainly about my Father.
(John 16:25)

I came from the Father and entered the world; now I
am leaving the world and going back to the Father.
(John 16:28)

After Jesus said this, he looked toward heaven and
prayed: "Father, the time has come. Glorify your
Son, that your Son may glorify you." (John 17:1)

Now this is eternal life: that they may know you, the
only true God, and Jesus Christ, whom you have
sent. I have brought you glory on earth by completing
the work you gave me to do. And now, Father, glori-
fy me in your presence with the glory I had with you
before the world began. (John 17:3-5)

Righteous Father, though the world does not know you, I know you, and they know that you have sent me. (John 17:25)

Jesus said, "Do not hold on to me, for I have not yet returned to the Father. Go instead to my brothers and tell them, 'I am returning to my Father and your Father, to my God and your God.'" (John 20:17)

Again Jesus said, "Peace be with you! As the Father has sent me, I am sending you." (John 20:21)

Jesus declared, "*If God were your Father, you would love me, for I came from God and now am here. I have not come on my own; but he sent me*" (John 8:42). He is addressing those who did not believe in Him. The root of their unbelief was not knowing the Father. If you don't know the Father, you cannot know His Son. Unbelief is caused by fatherlessness, not having a father.

Wayward children have no father. They have no respect for their elders, therefore, they cannot submit to authority. Children need to learn about the Father through fathers who teach them about God the Father.

A child needs to learn how God disciplines, teaches, instructs and does things through an earthly father who embodies the Father.

I thank God for my earthly father. He made certain that his children respected their elders. He taught me about authority. My father generated in me knowledge of what submission, authority and respect was all about. He was the source of my understanding about fathers because he knew the Father.

Unfortunately, there are many children today who do not have a father in the home. They don't have the benefit of a father to create within in them the honor and respect they need for other authority figures; therefore, they are cursing people on the streets, back-talking to their teachers, and utterly disrespecting their elders.

Without godly fathers creating in us a knowledge, respect, and fear of God, we are destined to be fatherless. By not knowing our real Father, we inevitably substitute a fraud and counterfeit for daddy. Jesus—speaking to the religious leaders of His day who rebelled against His teaching and questioned His identity, integrity, and legitimacy—said, *"You belong to your father, the devil, and you want to carry out your father's desire. He was a murderer from the beginning, not holding to the truth, for there is no truth in him. When he lies, he speaks his native language, for he is a liar and the father of lies."* (John 8:44).

Fathers create in their children what their fathers created in them. Remember, fathers are progenitors. They birth generations after them that are like themselves and their fathers. So if they are fatherless, their real father is the devil; therefore, they create generations that are like their stepfather, Satan, instead of like the Father, God. Satan is a "stepfather" with no legitimate, rightful claim to the children of men.

If you have the wrong father, you'll grow up with the wrong genes. A fatherless man births defective children. How are they defective? They are filled with what has been generated in them—sin, lies, and murderous hate.

Only the male man in Scripture is noted as being the source and progenitor of generations. So to Abraham, not Sarah, God said, *"I will establish my covenant as an everlasting covenant between me and you [Abraham] and your descendants after you for the generations to come, to be your God and the God of your descendants after you."* (Gen. 17:7). God does not indicate that Sarah is a progenitor. God promised her by saying, *"I will bless her and will surely give you a son by her. I will bless her so that she will be the mother of nations; kings of peoples will come from her"* (Gen. 17:16). Only the male man's seed can generate the conception of generations. Only the male has generating, creative power. He is the source, and the wife is the incubator.

Jesus knew that the Jews had become fatherless. They thought that Abraham was their father, failing to recognize that the God and Father of Abraham was their Source. The Jews did not start as a race of people with father Abraham. It was God, Abraham's Father, that called them into being. Like the Jews, we need to change fathers. We have lost our original father and his Father, and we follow a stepfather, the devil, with contaminated blood and genes filled with evil and ignorance.

Jesus wanted God's children to turn their hearts back to the Father and away from their stepfather (Satan). Everything Jesus did was to get us back to the Father. Notice that after His resurrection, Jesus said, *"I am returning to my Father and your Father, to my God and your God"* (John 20:17). Jesus is saying to us, "I have paid the price. I have shed My blood. I have descended into Hades, taken the keys, unlocked the door, and set the captives free. I have risen from the dead. My work is finished. I have created a new generation of children birthed by My Father and now your Father—God. Now I go to My Father and your's so that He can be your Father again."

Paul writes that we are "new creations" in Christ Jesus (2 Cor. 5:17). Jesus asserts that we must be born of water and the Spirit (John 3). Why? Through faith in Jesus, God has provided us a way to be set free from our stepfather and born anew into His family with God as our Father.

Jesus' mission of salvation was to have the children return to their Father. Isaiah prophesied this: *"For to us a child is born, to us a son is given, and the government will be on his shoulders. And he will be called Wonderful Counselor, Mighty God, Everlasting Father, Prince of Peace"* (Isa. 9:6). God knew that humanity needed both a Son to die and a Father to return us to God. Jesus was both the Son of man and the Everlasting Father. Humanity had a problem. We didn't know whose child He (Jesus) was nor who was His daddy.

JESUS SOLVED TWO PROBLEMS

Jesus came to us as a Son, a child of His Father, to show us how a child of God the Father should look, talk, and act. Jesus asserted, *". . . I do nothing on my own but speak just what the Father has taught me. The one who sent me is with me; he has not left me alone, for I always do what pleases him"* (John 8:28-29). So whoever saw Jesus, also saw the Father. (See John 14:9-11.) In Jesus, we learn what a child of the Father is like as well as what the Father is like.

> *Jesus came as the Everlasting Father to show us the Father and how to be like the Father.*

Isaiah revealed that the Son is the Everlasting Father (Isa. 9:6). His fatherhood requires us to be submitted and obedient to His every Word, because all that He says and commands comes straight from the Father. Men are transformed by the Spirit into the likeness of Jesus Christ (2 Cor. 3:18). In His likeness is the perfect image of being both a child of the Father and a father to children so that their hearts will be turned to the Father.

GOD THE FATHER AS PROGENITOR

Remember in the last chapter we saw that "father" is Ab or pater—the source, creator or progenitor. The prefix "pro" means to support and uphold. God is the Progenitor who creates all things and then supports and upholds them as the Father.

A father is one who generates, supports, and upholds the coming generations.

A progenitor is the source of everything that he supports and upholds. We receive genes from our parents. The genes are the source and substance of life itself. God is the Source of all genes, all substance, and all life. God is LIFE. Let's briefly explore this thought about genes.

Our genes determine skin color, certain physical characteristics, behaviors, emotional reactions or instincts, and how our thought patterns are processed. At the core of our natural identity are our genes. So when a man sows seed into the receptor (the woman) and a child is conceived, the next generation is given its identity by the seed and the genes.

Adam is the father of the human race. His genes were released into humanity. As the progenitor of humanity, what identity did humanity inherit from Adam? Death was passed on in Adam's seed.

Therefore, just as sin entered the world through one man, and death through sin, and in this way death came to all men, because all sinned. (Romans 5:12)

Remember, Cain was birthed a killer. The only inheritance we received from Adam was death. Since we are Adam's offspring in the natural, we need to change fathers as soon as possible. We need to be rebirthed with everlasting seed and genes by the Everlasting Father–Jesus.

In the Garden of Eden when Eve was tempted by the serpent, nothing happened. She picked the fruit, and nothing happened. She ate the fruit, and nothing happened. She swallowed the fruit, and nothing happened. But when she took the fruit to Adam–who was both her husband and her father–and he ate the fruit, the very next thing that happened was, *"Then the eyes of both of them were opened, and they realized they were naked"* (Gen. 3:7). Something went wrong. All hell broke loose. When the man ate the fruit, in his act of separating from the Father, all his children were contaminated–including his first child, Eve.

Exodus 20:5 reveals, *"You shall not bow down to them or worship them; for I, the LORD your God, am a jealous God, punishing the children for the sin of the fathers to the third and fourth generation of those who hate me."* Women are not identified as the ones who transfer sin; men are. So the only way to get rid of Adam's seed of sin is to renounce him and his stepfather (the devil) as your father. You have to renounce your family line and the generations of sin that have begotten you. Only the Second Adam (Jesus) can birth new life in you and break the curse of sin and death that you inherited from your natural father (Adam).

Adam did what many men still do today; he blamed Eve for his sin. Men are still blaming the women and mothers in our cultures for social problems with our children. The truth is that the root of our problems is fatherlessness.

Men, stop blaming women. Yes, Eve was deceived (1 Tim. 2:14), but Adam sinned, rejected his Father, and, through his seed, became the progenitor of sin to all forthcoming generations. *"Therefore, just as sin entered the world through one man [Adam], and death through sin, and in this way death came to all men, because all sinned"* (Rom. 5:12). The fall of man was the result of a father being sustained by his child. Eve gave to Adam. The resource gave to the source.

Adam, as progenitor, sowed his seed of rebellion against the Father into all generations, but Christ, as the Everlasting Father, sowed God's seed of life into all who would be born again. Renounce the father of all lies and return to the Father of light and life.

GOD THE FATHER AS SOURCE

Pater means source, sustainer, and nourisher. A father is both the source and sustainer of someone. Remember that a progenitor is a father who upholds and supports the coming generations. In addition to upholding and supporting, the father (pater) is the source.

Now, God did not choose to be Father; that's who He is by nature and function. All things were created by Him. Without Him was not anything made that was made (Gen. 1; John 1; Rom. 1).

As the Source of all that is, God was pregnant—if I may use that analogy—with the seen and unseen world. He carried the seed of the universe. As the Source, God the Father had everything in Him before anything was. So God created the entire universe and brought into being all that is from nothing (ex nihilo). The Hebrew verb for creating is "bara". The only proper subject for bara is "God", for only He creates. That which produces or creates is the source—i.e., pater, Ab, or father.

God is the Father of creation (Gen. 1; Isa. 63; John 1; Rom. 1; Eph. 3). As the Father of all spirits and angels (Eph. 3:14-15), God even created Lucifer. Lucifer and his hosts were angels that rebelled against God, but they were not created that way. They were created good but turned evil. Even the devil's existence is sustained by the Father. He could not exist without God's permission.

God sent forth His Word and created all that is. Paul writes that "He [the Word/Christ] is before all things, and by him all things consist" (Col. 1:17 KJV). All things were created by Him and for Him. So even the devil's creation came from the only source of all that is—God the Father.

Understand this: God does not tempt you, but He does allow Satan to test and tempt you. No temptation or trial comes your way that you cannot withstand. *"No temptation has seized you except what is common to man. And God is faithful; he will not let you be tempted beyond what you can bear. But when you are tempted, he will also provide a way out so that you can stand up under it"* (1 Cor. 10:13).

No demon or devil can come into your presence without permission from the Father. Though tempted and tested, Spirit-filled believers have the strength from the Father to overcome the enemy. Satan's source is God, and even the enemy is sustained by the Father. So the next time any temptation comes your way, remember that it comes by permission. In it, there will be something for you to learn and a way provided by the Father to overcome.

Consider it pure joy, my brothers, whenever you face trials of many kinds, because you know that the testing of your faith develops perseverance. Perseverance must finish its work so that you may be mature and complete, not lacking anything. (James 1:2-4)

In this you greatly rejoice, though now for a little while you may have had to suffer grief in all kinds of trials. These have come so that your faith--of greater worth than gold, which perishes even though refined by fire--may be proved genuine and may result in praise, glory and honor when Jesus Christ is revealed.
(1 Peter 1:6-7)

Through trials and tests, you will grow and come to understand more fully how God is the Source for everything you face in life.

In the next chapter, we will come to understand how God, as the Progenitor and Source, is also the Sustainer, Nourisher, and Protector. As the Source and Progenitor, God sustains all that He fathers or creates. He alone can bring something into existence, and He alone can sustain it.

Remember these key principles for knowing God the Father as Progenitor and Source:

- Sin is the result of a man—Adam—turning his back on his Father.
- Salvation is the result of a man—Jesus, the Second Adam—providing us with the way to return to the Father.

- Jesus knew the Father and became the Progenitor and Source of a new race of fathers who know the Father through the Son.
- We learn how God disciplines, teaches, instructs, and does things through an earthly father who embodies the Father.
- God is the Progenitor. He created everything and upholds and supports all that He created.
- Fathers are progenitors. They birth generations after them that are like themselves and their fathers. When a man is fathered by God, he produces godly fathers.
- As the Source, God the Father had everything in Him before anything was. Everything that is, was in God.
- Fathers are the source of instruction, information, and knowledge about God the Source.

Because fathers are the source, they must sustain, nourish, and protect all that comes out of them. That is our next topic, as we understand the functions of fatherhood.

Principles

- "Father" is the highest honor God bestows on man.

- The measure of a man's success is directly related to his effectiveness as a godly father, for which God is the ultimate standard and only true example.

- The source of sin is fatherlessness.

- Until men are restored to their position of fathering like the Father, families, communities, and nations cannot be healed.

- God has called men to be fathers like Him in order to turn the hearts of the children back to the Father. If you understand this principle and responsibility and begin to apply it in your life, then God will answer your prayers for provision, because He will father you as you also father your family.

- The level at which your child refers to you is the measure of your effectiveness as a father.

- Fathers are progenitors—the source that generates, supports, and upholds the coming generations.

3

FATHER AS SUSTAINER, NURTURER AND PROTECTOR

As I travel around the world, I see evil everwhere. At times, I ask the same question that Jeremiah asked, "*Why does the way of the wicked prosper?*" (Jer. 12:1). There are drug pushers, pimps, thieves, and dishonest business people everywhere who have big homes, cars, boats, and lots of money. What is the source of all that they have? How do they sustain their lives? The answer to those questions is the same answer as to why the righteous prosper. The Father (Sustainer) sends the rain upon the just and the unjust because everyone and everything is from Him (Matt. 5:45). If something comes from you as a pater (father), then you must sustain it even though it is rotten, no good, horrible and rebellious. Why? Because God is a good, faithful, and patient Father! He sustains, nourishes, and protects.

Jesus understood that with God as His Source, only good things could come from Him. The religious leaders criticized Jesus for doing miracles, saying that He was from the devil. Jesus answered His critics by saying, "*Which of you fathers, if your son asks for a fish, will give him a snake instead? Or if he asks for an egg, will give him a scorpion? If you then, though you are evil, know how to give good gifts to your children, how much more will your Father in heaven give the Holy Spirit to those who ask him!*" (Luke 11:11-13).

What has Jesus taught us? Simply this:

A father like the Father sustains, nourishes, and protects that which comes out of him as the source. God's sustenance does not depend on behavior or how it is received. He sustains what He creates because of His goodness.

Remember the parable of the lost son (more aptly called the parable of the loving father)? The ambitious and ungrateful son took his good inheritance, left home, squandered the inheritance, and ended up living in a pig's pen. It is important to note that while he was away from his home and his father, he still ate and drank in order to sustain his life, even if it was pig's food. Question: "Who created the food and water that the pigs ate?" The same Father–God. Therefore, despite his rebellious, separated state, the Father still sustained him on pig's food. God sustains everything and everyone He created, but the quality of the sustenance is determined by one's relationship to the Father. When the lost son returned home, the father still loved him and was willing to sustain him.

If you stay away from God, God will sustain you even with slop, if that's what you want. Why? You are still the son, and He is still the faithful Father. His faithfulness doesn't change just because you sin or rebel. God says, "I'll feed you slop if that's what you want to eat. The pigs and the garbage they eat are mine, and I will give them to you."

When the lost son came to himself, he said, *"How many of my father's hired men have food to spare, and here I am starving to death! I will set out and go back to my father . . ."* (Luke 15:17-18). In other words, he realized that the food in his father's house was better than the food in the pig pen. It's all food, but you can decide upon the quality of life you want to live just like the lost son did. God will feed you whatever you want to eat. If you hang out with the pigs, you will eat pig slop. If you return home to your Father, you can eat steak, wear fine clothes, and live in prosperity. The choice is yours. The Father sustains everyone because He is the Source and Creator of all. He sustains all things by the power of His Word.

One function of fathering is sustaining, nurturing, and protecting our children. That which comes from the source–the father–must also be sustained by the source.

GOD CREATED EVERYTHING TO SUSTAIN MAN

Everything we know about fatherhood begins at the beginning in Genesis–the Book of beginnings. In Genesis, God began humanity with one human. Out of the soil, He created everyone in the male man. He never went back to the soil to create anyone else. If father means the "source of a thing," then Adam was Eve's father. Remember, she was created out of Adam, not from the soil.

Follow this process of creation: God is the self-sustaining One. He doesn't use any stuff from any other source to create. God is the Source. Out of God comes the Word that speaks into being all the stuff of creation. Before the stuff of creation, Elohim–the name for God that means "many who are one"–decided to bring humanity into existence. *"For he chose us in him before the creation of the world to be holy and blameless in his sight. In love"*

(Eph. 1:4). God was pregnant with us before He created the universe. So the triune God, Elohim, decided to have sons, offspring, and spirit children who would be made in His image and likeness.

So God created us to be like Christ. In His purpose, supernatural womb, foreknowledge, and predestination, Elohim created His children. His plan for us was not only to be created in His image, but also to exercise authority and dominion just as He did. Since there was nothing for His children to rule, God spoke the universe into being. Creation, therefore, is the product of God's purpose for His children. In His foreknowledge, God spoke creation into being in order to sustain those begotten in His image.

I believe that in order for God to sustain the balance of the whole solar system, He created millions upon millions of galaxies, stars, and planets. God has made sure that creation will not wear out until He is finished with His purpose for us. God willed in eternity that His children would rule forever, so He created a universe that He will sustain forever.

This universe baffles scientists. The more they discover about it, the more they realize how little they know. The universe is bigger and greater than they ever imagined. Some say it is expanding. The truth is that it is infinitely greater than anything they can imagine because the infinite God created it for the man into whom He would breathe infinite, eternal life.

At the center of the universe's purpose is humanity. David's psalm declares, *"When I consider your heavens, the work of your fingers, the moon and the stars, which you have set in place, what is man that you [God] are mindful of him, the son of man that you care for him? You made him a little lower than the heavenly beings and crowned him with glory and honor. You made him ruler over the works of your hands; you put everything under his feet."* (Ps. 8:3-6). So the whole universe was created just for God's children to have a place to exercise the Father's dominion, and for their nature (image and likeness) to be like the Father. God created all that is, and thus became the Source, the Ab, and the Father of creation.

What is a father? One who produces something and then sustains it. Out of God the Father came the Word, His Son, who spoke all things into being.

> *"In the beginning was the Word, and the Word was with God, and the Word was God. He was with God in the beginning. Through him all things were made; without him nothing was made that has been made. In him was life, and that life was the light of men."*
> *(John 1:1-4)*

Not only did the Word create all that is, the Word also upholds, supports and sustains everything It created.

> *"But in these last days he has spoken to us by his Son, whom he appointed heir of all things, and through whom he made the universe. The Son is the radiance of God's glory and the exact representation of his being, sustaining all things by his powerful word."*
> *(Heb. 1:2-3)*

So out of the Father came the Son. God fathered His Son as the First Begotten.

> *"You are my Son; today I have become your Father"? Or again, "I will be his Father, and he will be my Son"? And again, when God brings his firstborn into the world, he says, "Let all God's angels worship him."* (Heb. 1:5-6)

The Son, as the Word, spoke all creation into being which would sustain humanity. The Father always sustains what He produces.

Now we have set the stage for Adam. In eternity, before time and creation, all humanity had been conceived in the mind of God. God created all things in order to sustain the man He would create in His image. So God finished everybody, put them in one body, and took that body–Adam–and put him in the Garden. God wanted everybody to come from one body, to have a source (father). Therefore, God put everybody in a male body.

So for eternity, the male is the father of human society and social relationships. He is the source of the human family. This puts an awesome responsibility on the man as a father. The male man, as a father, is the source, sustainer, nurturer, and protector of the woman.

In our society, too many women are called upon to do a father's job. Women were not created to be the sustainer. Too many men have abandoned their women and left them alone to sustain themselves and the offspring that the man gave her. Out of the man, God took the woman. (See Genesis 2.) He is the pater or source. Whatever is produced by a father must be sustained and nourished by it.

God did not go back to the soil to produce a woman. Why? He did not want the soil to support the woman. God made Adam to be a father. God wanted a father to represent Him on earth. Therefore, out of a father–Adam–was produced a woman to be fathered, sustained, and nurtured by the man. So God created man to be a father like Himself. The father is the source of the woman. Together, the man and woman came together in marriage. From the beginning God said, *"For this reason a man will leave his father and mother and be united to his wife, and they will become one flesh"* (Gen. 2:24). Notice that the Scripture never said that the wife leaves her father. Why? Because her husband is to be her father, her source, and her sustainer.

Out of man came the woman and marriage. Out of marriage came children. So there we have a family. When families gather together, we have a community. When a multiplicity of communities come together, we have a nation and a society.

FATHERS AS THE FOUNDATION

I want you to picture the problem with our nations and societies as well as the solution. God created man and out of him is produced a woman. Eve was Adam's baby. That means everything she needed to nourish and sustain her came from Adam, her source.

If societies and nations have problems with drugs, unwed mothers, teenage pregnancy, corruption, violence and the like, then they must go back to the foundation in order to solve the problem. If they have a national problem, then they must go back into the communities to find the problem. Obviously, the community's problems affect the nation, which is a multiplicity of communities. Community problems are rooted in the families that make up each community. So when we check to see what the family's problems are, we must look at marriages. When we examine the condition of our marriages, we discover that husbands and wives are divorced, mothers have been abandoned, and men are not sustaining their families. What does all of this boil down to? Brothers, we are at the root of the problem affecting the nations! The

foundational source has a problem . . . men are not being the fathers God created them to be.

The foundation of all societies is the male man.

Understand this: The church cannot fix society's problems when the foundation is out of place. *"When the foundations are being destroyed, what can the righteous do?"* (Ps. 11:3). No matter how much the church works at correcting social ills, if the foundation that God laid for the family is not in place, even the work of the righteous will not be successful. So the devil does not care if the church is filled with women. As long as men do not come to their Father, then women and their children are fatherless.

Fatherhood is the foundation of the family, the church, and the culture.

The primary mission of the church is to be fishers of men (Matt. 4:19; Mark 1:17). When men return to the Father, then they can be sustained and nurtured by their Source and become the sustainers they are called to be for their families. Remember, when humanity fell in Genesis 3, God never asked where the woman was. God asked, "*Adam, where are you?*" (Gen. 3:9).

In other words, Adam was out of position. The foundation had been shaken and destroyed. The whole of creation was unbalanced. God fathered Adam so that he could father and sustain Eve. Without fathers, the marriage, the family, the community, and the nation lay in shambles. A nation can only be sustained, nurtured, and protected when men are fathers like the Father.

Isaiah prophesied what would happen when men abandoned fatherhood and the foundations of the culture shattered. "*Youths oppress my people, women rule over them. O my people, your guides lead you astray; they turn you from the path*" (Isa. 3:12). When women rule, the whole nation, community, or household is in trouble.

Isaiah 3:4 describes a society or nation much like those in the world today in which women chase after men, men rule like mad children, and boys–not men–become leaders. Isaiah prophesied that there will be a scarcity of real men who are like God the Father. In such cultures, immorality and satanic oppression will be rampant. Men will become like women (receivers) and indulge in homosexuality. When such immorality sets in, women will rule men, and men will become like children. They will become feminized, responding to life like a woman.

Woman, when a man wants to marry you, do not ask him if he loves you; ask him who he loves. If his love for God is not his first priority, then he is a poor prospect for a fulfilling relationship. Refuse to form relationships with plastic men who melt when the heat and pressures of life get turned up high. Find someone who is real. Until you find a man who knows that God the Father is his Source and Sustainer, you must lean on Jesus; He will husband you until you find a man who can be a godly husband and father.

The protection that our society and families need is fathers. The Father created man. Out of man came the woman, marriage, and the family. The family must be sustained, nurtured and protected by men who are fathers. So, the family and the community are sustained and protected by fathers, and the nation ultimately must be sustained by fathers.

If an enemy wanted to destroy a nation, a community, or a family, who would the enemy attack? Just one person is the object of Satan's attack—the father! When fathers are moved out of their place as sustainers, nurturers, and protectors, the foundations are destroyed and the whole society crumbles.

For man did not come from woman, but woman from man; neither was man created for woman, but woman for man. (1 Cor. 11:8-9)

The Source and Sustainer of every man is Christ. It is time for churches to go after men and lead them back to the Father through Jesus Christ. When men get back to Christ, they return to their rightful position in creation as fathers like the Father. As fathers like the Father, men can then sustain their marriages, families, communities, and nations.

Men who are fathers like the Father are the unshakable foundation God purposed from the beginning by fathering Adam. In Christ, men return to their Source–God the Father–and then become sustainers, nurturers, and protectors.

The function of fathering like the Father who sustains, nurtures, and protects encompasses these principles:

- A father like the Father sustains, nourishes, and protects what comes out of him as the source.
- Creation is the product of God's purpose for His children. In His foreknowledge, God spoke creation into being in order to sustain those begotten in His image.
- God wanted everybody to come from one body, to have a source–a father. God put everybody in a male body–Adam.
- Everything to sustain women should come from their fathers or their husbands (who are also their fathers). The foundation for the whole human family is the male man.
- Fatherhood is the foundation of the family, the church, and the culture.

Now we will explore how a father really supports and raises up future generations in godliness and righteousness by fulfilling his function as the teacher.

Principles

- A father like the Father sustains, nourishes, and protects what comes out of him as the source— regardless of behavior or how it was received.

- God created man to be a father like Himself and to represent Him on earth.

- Out of man came the woman and marriage. Out of marriage came children and a family. Families create communities, and communities create a nation or society. Therefore, fathers are the foundation of all societies.

- Men who are fathers like the Father are the unshakable foundation God purposed from the beginning by fathering Adam.

4

FATHER AS TEACHER

Whatever we find in the first two chapters of Genesis is verified throughout Scripture and lays a foundation for understanding fatherhood, marriage, family, and culture. God gave Adam all the information that needed to be taught. Essentially, the Father teaches the father so that the father will teach the wife, children, and upcoming generations.

Then, God created the woman out of Adam. It is important to note that the Biblical record of Genesis gives no evidence that Eve received the instructions concerning the tree or the Garden directly from God; only Adam received direct instructions from God. God, therefore, made him responsible for teaching the woman and all that comes after him concerning what the Father said.

> *God teaches fathers and then*
> *fathers teach their household.*

This is clearly seen with Abraham. God said, *"Shall I hide from Abraham what I am about to do? Abraham will surely become a great and powerful nation, and all nations on earth will be blessed through him. For I have chosen him, so that he will direct his children and his household after him to keep the way of the LORD by doing what is right and just, so that the LORD will bring about for Abraham what he has promised him"* (Gen. 18:17-19).

The commands of God were taught by Abraham to his household and the generations after him. Therefore, if a man takes the responsibility to become the teacher and instructor in his home, he attracts God's favor and blessing. Why? Because the father being a teacher fulfills God's purpose for his life. Since the father is the source, then everyone who comes out of him must look to him for instruction. God teaches the father to teach the future generations.

Look again at Adam and Eve in Genesis 1-3. Eve was taken out of Adam. Eve was designed and fashioned to be a receiver, but she was receiving from the wrong source. Adam is the giver, obviously. So a female really is a receiver and an incubator. The woman does not initiate, she responds. She gives to her children as she has received from her husband who is also her father. So the man gives seed to the woman, and she gives back to the man a child. She takes what a man gives her, multiplies it, and gives it back. What incubators do is give life to the seed.

Herein lies a key principle: Whatever seed the father plants and whatever he teaches, that seed and instruction will be birthed through the mother to the children and the children's children. So, whatever Eve gave back to Adam was supposed to have been an increase and multiplication of that which Adam gave her in the first place. But, Eve broke the principle. She came to Adam with something he never gave her. She had received from a source other than the right source. God's purpose was distorted. God imparted to Adam. Adam instructed Eve, but Eve went to another source for teaching and instruction–the serpent. Consequently, instead of bringing back the fruit of life, Eve offered Adam the fruit of death.

Life comes from God the Father. Lies and destruction are what the devil gives. It is no wonder, then, that when Eve birthed children, the first fruit born by her children was hate and murder. She had received from a source not of God and birthed the thing she had received—death.

Let's apply this principle in our families. Our children are supposed to bring back to us all that we have deposited into them. The only way for a father to know how well he has done as a father is by his grandchildren. If the father has taught his wife and children the things of God, then godly lives will be produced in his children's children. But if the father is absent or fails to teach the principles and precepts of the truth from the Word of God, then sin will be the fruit of his children's children. It's that simple. That is the awesome power of the father as a teacher.

> *"Do not be deceived: God cannot be mocked. A man reaps what he sows. The one who sows to please his sinful nature, from that nature will reap destruction; the one who sows to please the Spirit, from the Spirit will reap eternal life."* (Gal. 6:7-8)

A wife and mother can only bear good fruit when the father sows into her the fruit of the Spirit. We see the results of sowing into the flesh all the time. Fathers that sow abuse, reap abuse. Fathers that sow addiction have addicted wives and children. Fathers that sow divorce, reap broken families. But fathers that sow the seed of the Spirit's fruit reap love, joy, peace, patience, gentleness, goodness, faith, meekness, and self-control. (See Gal. 5:22-23.)

Fathers are only to teach the truth they hear from the Father. As the perfect example of a teacher, the One called Everlasting Father (Isa. 9:6), Jesus, asserted, *"When you have lifted up the Son of Man, then you will know that I am the one I claim to be and that I do nothing on my own but speak just what the Father has taught me."* (John 8:28). All the Son taught about came from His Father, the Source. What a powerful force a father is in his family when his wife and children know that whenever he acts or speaks, he is hearing from God.

So the godly father doesn't react in anger toward his children by calling them names like fool, idiot, stupid or dumb. Why not? Because the Father never calls him those names. Rather, the godly father only speaks to his children what he has heard from the Father. So he calls his children saints, holy ones, priests, royalty, children of God, and sons of the Most High God. The father declares the image of God in Christ Jesus to his wife and children.

Remember the example of David and Solomon. Solomon did not teach his own wisdom but the wisdom he had learned from his father. *"Listen, my sons, to a father's instruction; pay attention and gain understanding. I give you sound learning, so do not forsake my teaching. When I was a boy in my father's house, still tender, and an only child of my mother, he [David] taught me [Solomon] and said, "Lay hold of my words with all your heart; keep my commands and you will live. Get wisdom, get understanding; do not forget my words or swerve from them."* (Prov. 4:1-5). The wisdom and truth David heard from God, he taught to Solomon.

THE FATHER INSTRUCTS AND THE MOTHER COMMANDS

"Listen, my son, to your father's instruction and do not forsake your mother's teaching." (Prov. 1:8). There is a difference between an instruction, command and law. Instruction is the giving or receiving of original informa-

tion for direction and function. A command is a repetition and enforcement of instruction. In a godly context, an instruction is the truth that a father has learned from the Father. He imparts that instruction to his wife. As a mother, she repeats what she has heard as a command. Growing up, that sounded something like this in my home: "Your father showed us how to mow the yard. Now when he left home this morning, your father told me to have you mow the yard. Go cut the grass." Dad gave the instruction, and Mom issued the law and gave the command. She repeated and enforced the instruction of my father.

Suppose I didn't keep my mother's law and ignored her commands. Know what happened? She would say, "Son, I am going to tell your father what you didn't do when he gets home." That's all she had to say. Immediately, I went and cut the grass. No questions were asked and no excuses were given, because I knew that behind my mother's command was my father's power and authority. He would bring judgment and discipline to my life if I failed to keep my mother's law.

The father's instruction is original information.
The mother's law or command is a repetition
of the father's original teaching.

This simple principle has been ignored in our society. We have homes in which the women are giving commands but never received instructions. So the children do not feel any authority nor sense any power in the voice of the woman because there is no man in the house. As a result, there is lawlessness and rebellion in the home in the behavior and attitudes of the children. The father is really the key to healing the whole society and fixing the family. In his family, he must return to his God-given function of being a teacher like the Father who teaches him.

Where, then, does the father get his original instruction and information? From the Father and His Word. Even if a father has not been fathered by a godly man, he is without excuse. He can return to the Heavenly Father and be saved. He can receive godly instruction from his pastor and righteous men in the church who know and love the Word of God. And of course, as a born-again believer, a father has the Holy Spirit within him teaching him everything that the Son hears from the Father (John 16:5-15).

So a father who does not have a godly father from whom he has learned the Word should get under the spiritual authority of a pastor who teaches the Word. Daily, a father should submit in his relationship with His heavenly Father. He now has the Heavenly Father—not an earthly father—to correct all of the things he lacks in his own life. Therefore, his family now has a teacher again.

THE TEACHER SPIRIT

The father is the Adam in the home. Fathers are built to teach; that explains why males have difficulty being taught by women. Instructions are supposed to come from the father. God created the man to give instruction and the woman to receive his teaching and then command the children. Even when men have nothing to teach, they hate to admit that they don't have the answers.

One of the problems that society has is that it believes the cliché, "I learned all that I know at my mother's feet." We should not be receiving instructions from our mothers. Solomon's approach is God's way. The father instructs, and the mother commands what the father has taught.

Once again, go back to the original foundation established in Genesis. It would have made no sense for Eve to have taught Adam about the tree of the knowledge of good and evil. She knew nothing about it. God the Father taught Adam, and Adam taught Eve.

Notice in Genesis 2:16-17 that, *"The LORD God commanded the man, You are free to eat from any tree in the garden; but you must not eat from the tree of the knowledge of good and evil, for when you eat of it you will surely die."* God commanded the man– Adam–what to do. We can discern from Genesis 3:1-3, that Eve knew about that instruction. How? Adam had taught her what God said; however, she allowed a source other than Adam to instruct her about the tree.

The father should teach his wife and offspring not to receive instructions from any source other than the Father.

Adam did a good job teaching Eve, but she started getting instruction from someone who was not her father. There is another lesson about teaching here. Eve was supposed to accept, obey, and believe what Adam, her source, had said, because Adam had received his information from the Father. However, she decided to forego what she heard from her father and began to receive and listen to the teaching of one who was not her father.

*This is a very important principle: If children can
learn to compare the information they receive
in books, magazines, and the media to God's
truth that they learned from their fathers,
then they can go anywhere and face anything
in culture and still know the truth.*

Although I encountered a myriad of diverse and
spurious philosophies in college, my father had already
spoken the truth rooted in the Father and His Word.
That truth became the standard by which I measured
everything. If Eve had compared what the serpent said to
what Adam had already told her, she would have known
immediately that the devil was lying. Instead, she accepted the serpent's lie without ever checking it against the
truth taught to her by Adam. She received instruction
from a source other than the Father and, consequently,
was deceived.

The godly father should always emphasize to his
wife and children that what he has learned is not only
from his earthly father but from his Heavenly Father. It's
the standard. A father like the Father desires that this be
said of him: "*As long as he lived, they [his family and descen-
dants] did not fail to follow the LORD, the God of their
fathers*" (2 Chron. 34:33).

As a father teaching my children, I am not serv-
ing my father but the God of my fathers. I am serving the
God of my spiritual fathers—Abraham, Isaac, Jacob,
Joseph, Moses, David, and the prophets. I am serving the
Father of my Lord Jesus Christ. So when my wife, chil-
dren, and grandchildren follow my teaching, they are fol-

lowing the Word of God. My children know that the credibility of what I teach isn't true just because I said it, but because God said it!

WHAT ABOUT SAVED WIVES AND THEIR UNSAVED HUSBANDS?

I hear some women in churches say, "I'm going to do this or that because the pastor said to do this or that. I'm going to do this area of ministry. I'm going to serve in this way. Now, my husband doesn't agree with me or believe I should do this, but I'm following God and my church, not my husband." How should this attitude be addressed?

The moment a woman takes a husband, she has become his offspring. Remember that Adam's baby was Eve. Adam said, *"The man said, "This [the woman] is now bone of my bones and flesh of my flesh; she shall be called 'woman,' for she was taken out of man"* (Gen. 2:23). Then the next statement in Genesis 2:24 reveals, *"For this reason a man will leave his father and mother and be united to his wife, and they will become one flesh."* It's important to note again that nowhere in Scripture does it say a woman should leave her father. Only the man leaves his mother and father. Both Jesus and Paul quoted this verse in their teaching about marriage. The implication is clear: Women never leave their fathers–only men do. Why? Because men are fathers. So when a woman is born into a home, she's under the authority of her father. When she gets married, she's under the authority of her other father, her husband. She goes from one father to another father because the male man–the father–is her source.

Paul affirmed this principle when he wrote, *"For man did not come from woman, but woman from man; nei-*

ther was man created for woman, but woman for man" (1 Cor. 11:8-9).

So when Paul writes that a man does not cover his head, he is speaking about authority (1 Cor. 11:1-16). Why? Because the man is the father, and the woman should be under the covering of authority. She should always be under a father. The father is for a woman both source and sustainer. Woman was created to receive, and man was created to give, instruct, and cover the woman.

Remember our question–what if a woman leaves her husband's authority to do what a church or pastor says? As a pastor, I cannot enter another man's house. He is his wife's husband, father, covering, and authority. I cannot instruct another woman to go against the authority of her husband. If I did, I would be acting as the serpent did in the Garden with Eve. Much correction in the church is needed here. Pastors and church leaders should never usurp the authority of husbands and fathers.

Take a perfect example of this situation. Jesus met the woman at the well (John 4). He's God and certainly could have worked a miracle, saved her, and instantly healed every area of her life, but He didn't. Why? He understood the principles and functions of fatherhood. So Jesus asked the woman a very simple question, yet we often miss the question. "Where is your husband?" He was dealing with her covering, authority, and father. Not even Jesus moved in to replace her husband. Her answer is interesting. She said, "I have no husband." Jesus' answer implied, "You are right. I know the ones you had, and the one you have now is not your husband. You are without a covering. I can help you. I can give you instructions."

So, what does a pastor or church do when a wife is under the authority of an ungodly man? In this area, the church has made many mistakes. Our ultimate goal in the church is not just to get a Christian woman into ministry. The goal of the church, according to Jesus, is to be fishers of men by going into all the world with the gospel. So God is more concerned about that woman's unsaved husband getting saved than that woman having a place in the church. The Great Commission in Matthew 28 is not to place people in positions. The Commission is to disciple the nations and save the world. Now, if that concept is clear, then we must do everything in our legal authority in the body of Christ to get that man saved. We should be encouraging and equipping the wife to witness to and love her husband as Christ loves her.

It contradicts the Great Commission for the church to compete with the woman's husband, whom they should want to win to Christ. So, when a woman comes to me as a pastor and says, "Pastor, my husband says I cannot come to the meeting that you called, but you are my pastor. What should I do?" My answer is, "You stay with your husband because I am not your father." And I even go so far as writing a note to her husband, apologizing for my program conflicting with his schedule, and requesting that he please forgive me. I send his wife back to him.

How might that husband respond? He may well be led to Christ because now he says, "I finally met a pastor who is not trying to compete with me." He will desire to know more about the God that his wife serves. Why? Because neither God nor the church tries to take his wife from him, but rather teaches her to love and respect him as her husband and the father of their household.

JESUS, THE RABBI AND TEACHER

One of the titles that Jesus has is Everlasting Father (Isa. 9:6). He is called by those around Him, rabbi or teacher. What qualified Him to teach? He is a father who receives His instructions from God, His Father.

Jesus, the Second Adam, succeeds where the first Adam failed. Jesus listened to the Father and only spoke what the Father said. He also taught exactly what the Father wanted taught. Out of Jesus comes a woman–the ecclesia, which means "those called out of." The bride of Christ, His Church, does only what He says because the bride has the Holy Spirit to speak only what the Son has heard from the Father (John 14-16). Notice the progression of teaching that Jesus defines, *"When the Counselor [Holy Spirit] comes, whom I will send to you from the Father, the Spirit of truth who goes out from the Father, he will testify about me. And you also must testify, for you have been with me from the beginning"* (John 15:26-27).

From the Father through the Son by the Spirit, we are taught the truth which we, in turn, teach others. So the only instruction we are supposed to speak should come from the Father. The Father, through Jesus–the Everlasting Father–gives instructions by the Holy Spirit to His bride, the church. Then the church takes the instructions from her Lord, Husband, and Everlasting Father, and speaks them out with authority as commands. This is the principle behind the statement of Jesus regarding authority and how we can use His name to command sickness, disease, demons, and mountains.

As the bride of Christ, the church has the Father's instruction, authority, and power to speak and act with boldness in the world. So we, the bride of Christ, are empowered to declare things. "I bind you" is a command, not an instruction. "I loose you" is a command. "Come out of him" is a command. The church binds, looses, heals, and delivers not as teachings, but as commands under the authority of our Teacher and Husband, Jesus Christ, who is the Everlasting Father.

One final point about the father's function as a teacher. Solomon said, *"Listen, my son, to your father's instruction [original information] and do not forsake your mother's teaching [commands of the original information]."* (Prov. 1:8). So a woman was not designed to give instructions, but to give commands, which means the woman's power is wrapped up in the man. The reason why the single mothers of our nations are having such a hard time is because they are giving commands but never receiving instructions. This is a key principle.

When I was growing up, there were eleven children in our family. One mother, one daddy, and eleven kids lived under one roof. My father worked all the time, but he was always at home in the voice of my mother. My mother never had to say, "If you don't do what I say, I will discipline you." All she had to say to keep the house in order was, "Do this and do that. If you don't, I will let your father know when he comes." In other words, she always had the authority of his instructions. My father would say to the children, "You wash the dishes today. You clean the floor. You mow the lawn." We would pray together as a family, and then he would go to work.

That's it. He didn't have to be home to assert his authority, because my mother was home. When she was in a meeting with some of her friends, all she had to do was look at me and say, "Myles, your father said to mow the lawn, so go mow the lawn now. Paul, wash the dishes and clean the floor." She was simply giving commands. When she said, "Mow the lawn," I didn't hear her, I heard my father! I knew that if I disobeyed her commands, I would also be disobeying my father, even though he was not physically present at that moment. My mother had the authority to say to me, "If you don't obey me, wait until your father comes home. He'll take care of you." That was enough! Believe me, I got the message. She invoked the authority of my father, and I had to comply, or else! A woman is designed to rule by delegated authority.

Christ does the same thing with His Bride. He gives us instructions, and He leaves. He leaves us in the world with His instructions. We go out and are supposed to possess the land and take back what the devil has stolen. We have the authority of the Father to do so. When we command, lives change because the authority of the Father is in us through His Holy Spirit. We declare truth in His name because we have His authority.

It is tragic that in many homes today, the mother cannot invoke the name of her child's father with authority. In fact, many curse the father's name. Why? Because the fathers have abandoned their responsibility to be teachers of the Word of God in their homes.

One of Satan's primary strategies is to remove fathers from the home. Satan hates fathers because when they do what they were created to do, they teach about the Father in their homes. Satan hates that! He wants the home to be in rebellion against fathers and the Father. If Satan can remove the teacher, then there is no instruction. If there is no instruction, there is no authority. If there is no authority, then there is anarchy and chaos. When there is anarchy and chaos, any number of undesirable things can happen—kids join gangs, get involved in drugs, and run with bad company because there is no authority in the home.

Since the father gives instruction in the home, he must also discipline and give correction to his household. We now turn to the father's function as the one who disciplines in the home.

Principles

- God teaches fathers, then fathers teach their households.

- Whatever seed the father plants and whatever he teaches, that seed and instruction is birthed through the mother to the children and the children's children.

- Earthly fathers are only to teach the truth they hear from the Heavenly Father.

- Fathers instruct, and mothers command; therefore, the father's instruction is original information. The mother's law or command is a repetition of the father's original teaching.

- The father should teach his wife and offspring not to receive instructions from any source other than the Father.

- Pastors and church leaders should never usurp the authority of husbands and fathers.

- As the bride of Christ, the church has the Father's instruction, authority, and power to speak and act with boldness in the world.

5

FATHER AS ONE WHO DISCIPLINES

Discipline is not punishment. Discipline takes teaching to the next level. It is one thing to teach a child, but correction and further instruction helps to shape a child's character. Discipline, therefore, is training.

"*Train a child in the way he should go, and when he is old he will not turn from it*" (Prov. 22:6). This instruction is spoken to fathers. Notice the application of this principle in Ephesians 6:4, "*Fathers, do not exasperate your children; instead, bring them up in the training and instruction of the Lord.*" Again, I want to emphasize that discipline is not punishment rendered by an irate or enraged father. Paul clearly warns, "*Fathers, do not embitter your children, or they will become discouraged*" (Col. 3:21).

What society has done is leave discipline to the women because most men think that training is punishment. In referring to woman, God said, "*The LORD God said, It is not good that the man should be alone; I will make him an help meet for him*" (Gen. 2:18 KJV). A help meet means to be "suitable" or "adaptable". One who is suitable or adaptable can be trained and equipped in responsibility.

In Genesis 2:15 KJV, "*The LORD God took the man, and put him into the garden of Eden to dress it and to keep it.*" Again, this refers to discipline and order. To "dress" means to cultivate, and to "cultivate" means to train.

A father is given by the Father the responsibility to train and equip everything under his care, including his wife and offspring.

What is the difference between cultivation and growth? When plants grow without cultivation, we call them weeds. Cultivated plants form a garden. Trees growing without cultivation and order are a forest. Cultivated trees are a grove. Without cultivation, there is no order, no decency, and no systematic development. But when there is training, order and planned development, we then see discipline and cultivation taking place.

God the Father loves cultivation. Genesis 2:5 reveals something very important. "*And no shrub of the field had yet appeared on the earth and no plant of the field had yet sprung up, for the LORD God had not sent rain on the earth and there was no man to work the ground.*" Even with all the wealth of the trees and plants in the earth, God didn't allow it to rain. Why? Because there was no man to cultivate the earth. Nothing grew on the face of the earth until there was a man to cultivate it.

God as our Father refuses to allow anything to grow without cultivation and training. He even withheld the rain because He did not want wild, unrestrained, and disorganized growth. God the Father has an orderly, disciplined, and purposeful plan for everything.

Part of God's purpose for man was to cultivate the earth given to him for sustenance. So then, God placed Adam in the Garden and gave him instructions to work, train, cultivate, and keep the earth. Part of man's job description was to dress and cultivate the earth. He kept creation according to God's purpose and order.

Likewise, the father is to keep and cultivate his creations–his offspring. When Eve came along and eventually the children, Adam, as a father, was to make certain that they did not grow wild. The world believes that children need to "sow wild oats" as they grow up, but that is a direct contradiction to God's plan of cultivation and discipline.

We have uncultivated and untrained boys throwing their seed–sperm–all over the place, and we are not cultivating, training, or disciplining them. Scripture never commands women to discipline and train, because that is the function of a father.

God the Father disciplines us, and fathers,
like God, discipline their children.

Hebrews says it this way: *"And you have forgotten that word of encouragement that addresses you as sons: 'My son, do not make light of the Lord's discipline, and do not lose heart when he rebukes you, because the Lord disciplines those he loves, and he punishes everyone he accepts as a son.' Endure hardship as discipline; God is treating you as sons. For what son is not disciplined by his father? If you are not disciplined (and everyone undergoes discipline), then you are illegitimate children and not true sons. Moreover, we have all had human fathers who disciplined us and we respected them for it. How much more should we submit to the Father of our spirits and live! Our fathers disciplined us for a little while as they thought best; but God disciplines us for our good, that we may share in his holiness"* (Heb. 12:5-10).

Let me give you some examples of the ways that fathers discipline, cultivate, and train their children. Also, remember that the word "discipline" comes from the word "disciple", which means one who learns by following. So fathers train, discipline, and disciple their children by having them follow their example. That is exactly what Jesus had his disciples do. He told them, "Follow Me!"

> *When fathers train their children, they teach by example. It is then that their children should learn by imitation.*

A concrete example of this is a train. We mistakenly call an entire line of cars on a track a "train". However, only the engine is the train, because everything else attached to the engine is a follower. The principle that governs an automotive train is the same principle God wants implemented in our families.

A father is never supposed to just point his wife or children in a direction. He is the engine, and should be able to say, "Hook up to me. Go where I am going. Follow me. Imitate my example, and then you'll be going in the right direction."

A father's primary responsibility is to be like the heavenly Father and to do what He does. God does not point one way then go another. A true father never says, "Do what I say but not what I do." Instead, a godly father with integrity can unashamedly say to his wife and children, "Live the way I live, and you will be like the Father." In other words, a father becomes in Christ what he wants his wife and children to become.

Consider Abraham's example. Abraham received favor from God because Abraham cultivated his household in the commandments of God (Gen. 18). He even cultivated his servant. He did not allow anyone to work in his household without being trained and disciplined in the ways of God. He made certain that even his servants obeyed God's standards and followed his example. The principle is this:

A father follows the example of the Father and teaches his offspring to follow him. A godly father leads everyone following him to the Father.

Abraham did not want a pagan working for him. Everyone in his household followed father Abraham, and Abraham followed God the Father.

Fathers must become disciplinarians. They must *disciple* their families. A disciple is a follower who learns by observation. That's why disciples in the past always left home because learning was *living* life, not just talking about it. The father not only teaches in the home, but he also takes his children out into the world with him in order to have them observe how he handles different situations in a godly way. So if a father is going to discipline his children, then he must also disciple his children and take them to see how he functions under different conditions and situations.

You cannot disciple on the telephone or via e-mail. That's foolishness. Trying to disciple a child while not being there makes a man a biological supplier of sperm, not a father. A father trains a child by having the child observe what the father does, says, and decides in the real world.

Fathers need to discipline and disciple their households by letting their families observe them:

- Reading and applying the Word of God.
- Praying and interceding.
- Making right decisions based on the principles and absolute truths of God's Word.
- Working in the real world, living out the example of Christ.
- Sharing the gospel with others.
- Worshiping and praising God the Father openly.
- Handling and solving problems without compromise.
- Being promise keepers and not promise breakers.
- Treating their wives with honor and dignity.
- Honoring others above themselves.
- Loving their enemies.
- Being reconcilers between races and economic classes of people.
- Making sure that their words and actions correspond—exhibiting character and integrity.

In ancient Israel, the disciples followed their rabbis everywhere, learning to live by the rabbi's example. When fathers disciple their children, they show them how to live life by their example. So the father becomes a master in his own household; that is not a negative description. As the father masters the skills and gifts of operating in the power of the Spirit, the family can observe the master and learn for themselves how to walk in the Spirit.

It is impossible to be a long-distance father.
A father cannot father children he is not with
nor train children who are not by his side.

Since the father as one who disciplines has his household follow his example, then our next step toward understanding the functions of fatherhood will be to examine how the father is the head and leader of his home.

Principles

- Fathers are given by the Father the responsibility to train and equip everything under their care.

- God the Father disciplines us, and godly fathers discipline their children.

- When fathers train their children, they teach by example, thereby enabling their children to learn by imitation.

- Fathers cannot father children they are not with nor train children who are not by their side.

- A father follows the example of the Father and teaches his offspring to follow him. A godly father then leads everyone following him to the Father.

- Fathers need to disciple their households by allowing their families to observe them operating in a godly manner and in the power of the Spirit

6

FATHER AS HEAD AND LEADER

A Latin word for father is "fundus", which means base or bottom, from which we get our word "foundation". The foundation of the family is the father who begins as the progenitor and source and then sustains, nourishes, protects, teaches, and disciplines his household.

As the foundation, the father is the head of the family as a result of God's timing and creation. Now the fact that he is the head does not mean that he is superior, better, or greater than the woman. It means he has first responsibility and accountability for the family.

Being the head is not a value statement about worth or intrinsic value. The father can never say that being the head or leader makes him the greatest. Jesus as Head of the church humbled Himself as a servant: *"Your attitude should be the same as that of Christ Jesus: Who, being in very nature God, did not consider equality with God something to be grasped, but made himself nothing, taking the very nature of a servant, being made in human likeness"* (Phil. 2:5-7).

Heads and leaders are first and foremost servants like Christ. It is impossible to assume a position of leadership without first serving.

You know that those who are regarded as rulers of the Gentiles lord it over them, and their high officials exercise authority over them. Not so with you. Instead, whoever wants to become great among you must be your servant, and whoever wants to be first must be slave of all. For even the Son of Man did not come to be served, but to serve, and to give his life as a ransom for many. (Mark 10:42-45)

We can use the physical head as an analogy for understanding the spiritual functions of being the head of the family. As the head of the family, the father is responsible for the body. Many men love to say, "I'm the head of this house," but they forget the responsibility and duty of being the head. The head has the responsibility to preserve, protect, nourish, and guide the body.

FATHERS PLAN

First, the head contains the brain. If the man claims to be the father and the head of the home, then he must have the mind of Christ (1 Cor. 2:16), which contains the knowledge and wisdom he needs to lead a family in the ways of God. The father has the responsibility to solve the problems that the family encounters. He calculates where the family is going and seeks God's guidance to make long-term plans—10, 15, or 20 years—for the family. The father is the counselor, career and financial planner, and manager of the family resources. All of those functions are in the brain. Fingers and legs do not make those kinds of decisions, because those decisions are made in the brain.

FATHERS PROVIDE VISION

The father, if he is truly the head, becomes the visionary of the family. The eyes are in the head and they see what's in front of the body. The eyes are not in the back or in the stomach; they are in the head. If you are the head, you are supposed to have a vision for your family—insight, long-range goals, and a plan for the future. The father discerns things that are happening in the natural as well as the supernatural for the family.

As the visionary, the father anticipates things before they happen and prepares and equips the family to face the future. Fathers have perception, conception, and inception.

- **Perception:** Awareness of what's going on. A father knows what's happening with his wife and children at all times. When behaviors or attitudes change, he knows it. When spiritual or physical needs arise, he is aware of them. Nothing escapes his attention. The father is tuned into and cares about each person in his family. Too often I hear families complain, "Dad just isn't with it. He never knows or understands what's happening in our lives. He's too wrapped up in his work to notice us." Remember, God cares about everything. Jesus noticed everything that happened around Him, even to the point of noticing a woman in need barely touching the hem of His garment (Mark 5). God the Father is aware of all things. Jeremiah prayed, *"Great are your purposes and mighty are your deeds. Your eyes [God]* are open to all the ways of men; you reward everyone according to his conduct and as his deeds deserve." (Jer. 32:19). Like the Father, a father perceives (is aware of) all that happens in his family.

- **Conception**: The creative beginning of a process; setting in motion a chain of events. God the Father sets everything in motion. *"The God who made the world and everything in it . . ."* (Acts 17:24). God the Father initiates, conceives, and creates. The father conceives in his mind the beginning of things for the family and then becomes the source for bringing what he has conceived into reality. As the head of the family, he takes the initiative to listen to God and conceive *God's* ideas, not just what seems like good ideas for the family.

- **Inception:** The start or commencement of some- thing new. God the Father is always doing a new thing in our lives. *"See, I [God] am doing a new thing! Now it springs up; do you not perceive it? I am making a way in the desert and streams in the wasteland"* (Isa. 43:19). A father is willing to risk new things with his family. He will break out of old traditions and bondages. A father receives the news that God has for him and his family, rejoicing in the refreshing newness of God's river in his life.

FATHERS DISCERN

What else is in the head? The nose. The nose dis- cerns. Are you a father who is always discerning? Now discerning actually has to do with caring. To care means to anticipate a need and meet it. A godly father can sense what is coming against a family in the next ten years. He can prepare for the future. He has a sense of what is going to happen next week. Perhaps his teenager may be going through some tough changes and tremendous peer pressure. As the head of the household, he discerns the problem and spends time with that child to counsel, support, affirm, and advise; he is discerning what is going on in his children. A godly father also senses when his wife is in need of a hug and affection. In other words, a father has a sense of smell. He can smell the scent of his family, his home, his business, and his neighborhood.

God the Father prepared for us before the foundation of the world. Read this:

Praise be to the God and Father of our Lord Jesus Christ, who has blessed us in the heavenly realms with every spiritual blessing in Christ. For he chose us in him before the creation of the world to be holy and blameless in his sight. In love he predestined us to be adopted as his sons through Jesus Christ, in accordance with his pleasure and will—to the praise of his glorious grace, which he has freely given us in the One he loves. In him we have redemption through his blood, the forgiveness of sins, in accordance with the riches of God's grace that he lavished on us with all wisdom and understanding. And he made known to us the mystery of his will according to his good pleasure, which he purposed in Christ, to be put into effect when the times will have reached their fulfillment--to bring all things in heaven and on earth together under one head, even Christ. In him we were also chosen, having been predestined according to the plan of him who works out everything in conformity with the purpose of his will, in order that we, who were the first to hope in Christ, might be for the praise of his glory.

And you also were included in Christ when you heard the word of truth, the gospel of your salvation. Having believed, you were marked in him with a seal, the promised Holy Spirit, who is a deposit guaranteeing our inheritance until the redemption of those who are God's possession--to the praise of his glory.
(Eph. 1:3-14)

God prepared for Christ to die for our sins, for the earnestness of the Holy Spirit, and for our eternal inheritance in glory. Now that's a real father! God was sniffing out our need before we were ever created. Jesus was sensing our need before His crucifixion and resurrection. He said, *"And if I go and prepare a place for you"* (John 14:3).

Consider Adam in the Garden before Eve was created from him. God anticipated man's loneliness. Adam didn't know he was alone. He had the Garden, all the creatures of the earth, and most of all, he had God. Adam could not have possibly been lonely because he dwelt within God's presence; however, God knew the purpose and nature of the man He created. God the Father anticipated Adam's need before he even had it; therefore, God created Eve.

The father discerns (sniffs out, smells, and senses) the needs of his family.

FATHERS LISTEN

Located on the head are also the ears. You are a father if you can hear for your family. The father should always be listening to God and to his family, for God the Father always listens to us. I hear wives and children continually complain, "Dad never has time to listen to me."

Fathers, please take time to listen. As a father and head of the family, here are some questions you need to ask yourself:

- Are you hearing the voice of God?
- Are you getting instructions for yourself and for the family's sake?
- Are you getting information for the children and for your wife?
- Are you picking up on what's going on in the world and preparing your family to face it?
- Are you hearing correction and instruction and rebuke?
- Are you hearing the true voice of your wife and children?

Many men think that they are too busy to listen to their families. Listening is a gift that fathers give to their families. When men listen, their listening tells their families that they care for them.

Failure to listen communicates a lack of love and caring for a family. Because the Father loves us, He always listens to and answers us. Fathers like the Father listen!

If they want to inquire about something, they should ask their own husbands at home; for it is disgraceful for a woman to speak in the church. (1 Cor. 14:35)

FATHERS SPEAK THE WORD OF GOD

Finally, being the head of the family means that the father is the mouthpiece for the family. That means the father is supposed to speak the Word of God in the home.

Through the father's voice,
the family hears God's voice.

If the children want to hear what God is saying, they shouldn't go to somebody else. If a wife wants to hear from God, she should hear from her husband, who is also her husband—not the pastor, prophet, apostle, teacher or evangelist in the church. The family should hear God's Word from the head of the family first. Everything said at church should confirm and support what has already been said first at home by the father.

For example, Paul said that women should be silent in the church.

> *"Women should remain silent in the churches. They are not allowed to speak, but must be in submission, as the Law says. If they want to inquire about something, they should ask their own husbands at home; for it is disgraceful for a woman to speak in the church."*
>
> *(1 Cor. 14:34-35)*

It is important to understand the full context of this Scripture in order to appreciate the true value and impact of Paul's admonition.

In the church meetings at Corinth, there were many problems because some of the people who converted to the Christian faith came from prostitution and pagan practices; therefore, some of the services were at risk of becoming wild or uncontrollable if those new converts reverted to their old pagan practices. Furthermore, in the synagogues, men and women were separated. The men would sit in the main area while the women sat behind them or in a balcony. In this setting, many women would ask their husbands questions about what the rabbi was teaching by speaking through a grill or making noise from the balcony.

Firstly, Paul was saying that God wants order and decency in the church. Secondly, it was not culturally in order for a woman to speak in public. And thirdly, Paul knew that when the wife went home, she should then ask her husband to answer her questions about what had been taught. The implication is that the husband should know the answer. In fact, the husband should have anticipated his wife's questions and taught her the Word or law before she went to synagogue.

Yes, a woman has ministry gifts and should exercise them. The problem with women speaking in the church was a male problem. When fathers and husbands fulfilled their responsibilities as the heads of the home, then women did not have to ask questions in the midst of a service; they received their answers from the head of the family who spoke with God's voice to the family.

THE FATHER AS LEADER

Being the head of the family does not impart more worth or value to the man. Being the head has to do with responsibility. Too many men confuse being the head with being the boss. A father is not the boss of his house; a father is the head. A father doesn't rule his house; he leads his house. Therefore, we must understand the function of the father as leader in the home.

A father doesn't dominate or control his house. He develops the potential of everyone in his house through his leadership.

Let me share with you some qualities of leadership that the father has in the home:

- As leader, the father has a passion and desire to bring out the best in all of those under his care—his wife, children, and any other family members.

- A true leader does not suppress, oppress, or depress the potential and talents of others; he releases them and cultivates them.

- A true leader provides an environment for growth. He does not try to inhibit family members or create an atmosphere of fear. A true leader's passion is to maximize the potential of others in order for them to realize their full and true abilities and eventually work himself out of a job.

- A true leader cultivates. In a very true sense, a father does exactly what God said from the beginning—he cultivates. To cultivate means to create an orderly environment that brings out the best in a thing; to culture it. As a leader, the father cultivates, develops, expands, instigates, motivates, inspires, encourages, and exhorts. All of those functions cultivate the soil in which others grow.

"I am the true vine, and my Father is the husbandman." (John 15:1 KJV)

Jesus taught that the Father is the Husbandman of the vine—the church. Just as God, the Husbandman, cultivates the vine so that it can grow, so the father, like God, cultivates his family as the head and leader. Jesus is the Head of the church, His bride. He loves and gives Himself for her. In the same way, the father, as head of the family, loves and gives himself daily for his wife and children.

> *"Instead, speaking the truth in love, we will in all things grow up into him who is the Head, that is, Christ." (Ephesians 4:15)*

> *"For the husband is the head of the wife as Christ is the head of the church, his body, of which he is the Savior." (Ephesians 5:23)*

Now, let's turn our attention to the caring function of the father for his family. As head and leader of the family, the father also deeply cares for his family in every area of their lives.

Principles

- Heads and leaders are first and foremost servants like Christ. It is impossible to assume a position of leadership without first serving.

- As the visionary, the father anticipates things before they happen and prepares and equips the family to face the future. Fathers have perception, conception, and inception.

- Listening is a gift that fathers give to their families. When men listen, their listening tells their families that they care for them.

- Through the father's voice, the family hears God's voice.

- A father doesn't dominate or control his house. He develops the potential of everyone in his house through his leadership.

7

FATHER AS ONE WHO CARES

In many ways, the father's funtions of caring and developing go hand-in-hand. Caring is also rooted in Genesis 2:15 KJV, *"And the Lord God took the man, and put him in the Garden of Eden to dress and to keep it."* The word "dress" in that verse means to cultivate and care for. To care is to pay close attention to needs and to also meet those needs. In fact, caring goes far beyond our normal thoughts of serving, encouraging, and ministering to someone.

Again, the word "care" means to anticipate a need and meet it. In other words, to care means that you calculate the next need of a person before they are aware they are going to need it; you make provisions immediately before they sense the need for it. That is the kind of caring that Psalm 8:4 describes, *"What is man that you are mindful of him, the son of man that you care for him? "* To be mindful means to have one's mind filled with thoughts about another person. God the Father has filled His thoughts with us. In other words, He anticipates and thinks about what we need before we even need it.

Jesus teaches us that our Father cares deeply for us. He says, *"So do not worry, saying, 'What shall we eat?' or 'What shall we drink?' or 'What shall we wear?' For the pagans run after all these things, and your heavenly Father knows that you need them*" (Matt. 6:31-32). The Father knows our needs and cares.

A father like the Father cares by spending his time and energy anticipating what his wife and children need next. This is the most beautiful picture in the world of a father. No matter what he is doing, he is constantly thinking about what his daughter will need next, what his son will need next year, or what his wife will need next week. He's constantly thinking about caring for his family.

Our work-driven cultures try to force men to continually think about what the company or corporation needs. Men no longer work to live, but live to work. Even when at home, a man's mind can be seen drifting off to work and either solving work problems or thinking of new work projects. Or, the father comes home so tired from working so much that he dozes off in front of the television. Meanwhile, his family goes neglected and not cared for because he is too tired or busy to think about their needs.

> *Fathers need to set right priorities. A father who cares like the Father thinks of his wife first, his children second, and his job third.*

A father should see his job as being a gift from God to care for his wife and children. In other words, God's care has provided the man with a job so that he can adequately care for the physical needs of his family. The job is a means to an end, never the end itself.

So these men who are wrapped up in their careers and running after the corporate world have their motivation and priorities out of place. They have taken their work, a gift from the Father that He intended to help care for their families, and made an idol out of it. They end up caring more about the gift than the family for which it was given or the God who gave it. Such idolatry will ruin the man and his family.

PASTORS AS FATHERS

One model that our churches often look up to for fathering is the pastor. I want to address a concern I have about pastors modeling fatherhood for their people. In our society, pastors have a growing divorce rate. Many could be properly classified as "workaholics". Often, pastors' wives feel helpless in trying to turn their husbands' hearts back toward home. The pastor seems to care for everyone else before his family. To defend their workaholism, pastors may say to their wives, "You know I'm doing this for the church. This is my calling. I'm doing this for the Lord." Unable to compete with God, the families desperately try to get their needs met inappropriately and may even end up blaming God for their fathers caring more for the church than for their families. The church then becomes a mistress to the pastor, as he leaves wife and family to suffer without him.

Lay people also need to know what I am about to say and take it to heart, for they often are a major cause of the pastor's problems. They expect the pastor to be Christ and not simply the pastor. The man of God can never take the place of Christ caring for His bride. Lay people turn too often to the pastor to meet their needs instead of to the Lord. As a result, the demands on the pastor's counseling, calling, and visitation become unrealistic. Only Christ is omnipresent, omniscient, and omnipotent—not the pastor.

So the answer to this dilemma is very simple and clear. It's found in Ephesians 5 where the principles are laid down by Paul concerning Christ and His wife, and the husband and his wife. Here's a statement Paul said that I think wraps it up: "*Husbands, love your wives, just as Christ loved the church and gave himself up for her*" (Eph. 5:25).

> *Pastors are to love their wives as Christ loved the church. Scripture never says that pastors are to love His wife, the church.*

Today, some church pastors are committing adultery with the church. They are trying to love the wrong woman. As a pastor, I am not married to my church today; I'm married to my wife. The woman that I oversee once in a while is not my wife–that's His wife. Who meets the church's emotional needs? Not me. Who meets her physical needs? Not me. Who meets her temporal needs? Not me. Who meets her spiritual needs? Not me. Christ meets all the needs of His wife, the church. Some pastors are destroying their own wives because they are trying to take over another Man's wife.

As far as the church is concerned, pastors should be the prime examples of fathers caring for their families. One of the reasons we have so many broken homes among pastors is that they cared more for their work than their family. We see pastors' children who are wayward, disoriented, confused, and backslidden because the pastor was not a father. He did not care for his family, and he tried to live with another Man's wife.

Husbands, love your wife like Christ loves His wife. Jesus never said love His wife. As a matter of fact, nowhere in the Bible does it say, "Love the church." It says, "Love your own wife" all throughout Scripture.

A father's care is one of his major functions. He sits down and calculates the upcoming needs of his family and then plans and works to meet those needs.

Finally, let's turn to the function of fathering as the one who develops his family.

Principles

- A father like the Father cares by spending his time and energy anticipating what his wife and children need next.

- Fathers need to set right priorities. A father who cares like the Father thinks of his wife first, his children second, and his job third.

- Pastors are to love *their* wives as Christ loved the church. Scripture never says that pastors are to love *His* wife, the church.

- A man's job is a gift from the Father that He intended to help care for that father's family. When a father places more importance on his work than his family, he makes an idol out of his work and will bring ruin upon himself and his family.

8

FATHER AS DEVELOPER

The father develops his family. To develop means to cause to grow gradually and continually in fuller, larger, and better ways. God the Father develops His people. Consider what Paul said about the Father: *"I [Paul] planted the seed, Apollos watered it, but God made it grow. So neither he who plants nor he who waters is anything, but only God, who makes things grow. The man who plants and the man who waters have one purpose, and each will be rewarded according to his own labor. For we are God's fellow workers; you are God's field, God's building."* (1 Cor. 3:6-9).

THE CHARACTERISTICS OF DEVELOPMENT

To understand the father as developer, we return again to the Garden and remember God instructing Adam to dress and keep the Garden of Eden (Gen. 2:15). In dressing and keeping the Garden, Adam had to plan for the orderly growth of both plant and animal life. Developing for order and cultivation started when Adam named the animals (Gen. 2:19-20).

Development has certain characteristics:

- *Planning.* Inherent in God's purpose is His plan. Before a developer starts building a housing division or shopping complex, he has a plan. He presents the plan to the appropriate governmental officials in order to obtain the required permits to build. The plan includes what will be constructed as well as how it will be used. Structure and usage are essential to a plan. For example, the Father as Developer planned the Garden and also planned what would be in it. He then determined what could and couldn't be used in the Garden and gave specific usage instructions to Adam. God structured a river to flow through the Garden and mist to come up from the earth in order to sustain the Garden. He provided food for Adam and Eve to eat and had a plan concerning what they could eat. " *Then God said, "I give you every seed-bearing plant on the face of the whole earth and every tree that has fruit with seed in it. They will be yours for food . . . And the LORD God commanded the man, "You are free to eat from any tree in the garden; but you must not eat from the tree of the knowledge of good and evil, for when you eat of it you will surely die*" (Gen. 1:29; 2:16-17).

- *Preparing and Planting.* Once there is a plan, the developer begins the necessary groundwork for building. Earth movers come in and drainage is developed. The land is prepared to accept the building—first a foundation and then a framework. Likewise, a sower prepares the soil and sows the seed in planning for a harvest. God the Developer *"Now the LORD God had planted a garden in the east, in Eden; and there he put the man he had formed."* (Gen. 2:8).

- *Protecting.* Every developer protects his construction site. He may construct a tall fence with barbwire to keep out intruders. He may hire security guards. Also, the farmers who develops a crop uses whatever means of protection his crop needs to guard against insects, diseases, and vandals. He tends the group by pulling weeds and providing adequate irrigation. God the Developer protected man by warning him about not eating from the tree of the knowledge of good and evil and giving him instructions on what to do in the Garden. God also walked with Adam and Eve in the cool of the evening (Gen. 3:8). Being in His presence was protection for Adam and Eve.

- *Producing.* Once a building is finished, the developer uses his shopping complex, houses, or commercial building to produce income. The farmer grows a crop and doesn't just leave it in the field. He has a harvest because the crop has produced fruit which can be used and sold. The Father develops us to be productive in His plan and purpose. Jesus addressed this issue of development very specifically: *"This is to my Father's glory, that you bear much fruit, showing yourselves to be my disciples."* (John 15:8).

Like the Father, an earthly father develops his wife and children. He plans their growth in every aspect of life–physically, intellectually, emotionally, and spiritually.

A father walks each step of the way with his family as he prepares and equips them in the ways of God. He plants the seed of God's Word in their hearts. He protects them with prayer and with his presence and provision for their lives.

> *A godly father walks with his family and is an example of holiness for them. He expects the best for them in producing good fruit, which gives glory to the Father. He develops his offspring to glow with the glory of God. A father expects his family to be the light of the world, salt of the earth, and witnesses for Christ in the world.*

Light produces light. The light of Christ in a father's life sets his family ablaze for Christ. Hebrews describes how the Father had His first begotten Son come into the world and make *"his servants a flame of fire"* (Heb. 1:7). Such is the prayer of every godly father–that his children become flames of fire, blazing with the Father's Spirit and shining as stars (Dan. 12:3).

THE ENVIRONMENT FOR DEVELOPMENT

As a father develops his offspring, he disciples them by providing an example of the Father. He encourages steady, consistent, and progressive growth in his family. For example, he will not give answers all the time but will show his children where to find the answers.

> *A father like the Father encourages discovery and learning as part of the developmental process.*

Development creates an environment that is conducive to others encountering learning experiences under the guidance of a father's godly wisdom. So what does an environment that encourages development and growth look like? Let me share with you some qualities of a father who develops his offspring:

- *Encouragement.* The father edifies his offspring. *"Therefore encourage one another and build each other up, just as in fact you are doing."* (1 Thess. 5:11). Fathers never tear down the esteem of a family member. Paul writes that God gave him power to edify not destroy (2 Cor. 13:10). Such is the power that God gives fathers–to build up their families, not pull them down.

- *Positive feedback.* Instead of criticism, a father like the Father gives constructive correction. He develops his wife and children by building on their strengths and focusing on what they can do well, instead of condemning them for their weaknesses. In fact, the father bears the weakness of his family (Rom. 15:1). He covers–not exposes–their vulnerability, and he protects them from an attack with his own prayers and instructions. Remember that Job built a hedge about his family to protect them from any evil they might bring upon themselves (Job 1:5).

- *Opportunity to try and fail.* Fathers understand that some of the most significant learning experiences that occur in life result from failure. Children can learn from their failures if a father uses the failures for teaching and correction instead of judgment and punishment. A father develops an atmosphere of acceptance for his family. He will not reject them just because they tried and failed. He accepts his family "for better or worse," just as Christ has accepted him. *"Accept one another, then, just as Christ accepted you, in order to bring praise to God."* (Rom. 15:7).

- *Does not make comparisons.* A father understands that the only standard for life is Jesus Christ. He never compares his wife or children to others, thinking that by forcing a comparison, he will force improvement. A father never says, "Son or daughter, why can't you be more like so and so? They are such good kids and never cause their parents any trouble. They make such good marks in school; why can't you?" Or, "Wife, why can't you dress and look like so and so? She is such a good cook and helpmate. Why can't you be more like her?" Such comments by a father come from the father of lies. Satan desires that we compare ourselves and families to others so that he can divide families and conjure up strife. When we compare ourselves to Christ, we all fall short of His glory. Everyone needs grace. Even as He gives grace to us, we must impart grace to others. Paul warns against comparison (2 Cor. 10:12). Every family member is a unique child of God. So, fathers like the Father are not respecter of persons (Acts 10:34). They develop an atmosphere in the family of mutual love, respect, honor, and caring for one another.

So, a godly father is constantly developing his family to grow into God's limitless potential, to be their best through His strength, and to accept others as they are growing in Christ.

A husband is there to develop the best in his family. He stretches his wife and children to achieve their utmost for His highest. He continually tests the character and abilities of his children. When helping them with their homework, he will not give them the answers but will help them learn how to solve the problems. When facing tough decisions, he will not always tell them what to do, but he will teach them right from wrong and how to make godly decisions based on the nature and character of the Father.

The objective of development is permanent growth.

The father cultivates his relationship with his wife and children so that they will grow beyond themselves and into the saints God purposed them to be. The powerful message of 2 Corinthians 5:17 is that new creations in Christ are continually having old things—sin, bad habits, ignorance, and strongholds—pass away, while all areas of life are becoming new. Fathers understand that God's children are always becoming! We are developing and growing into Christ's image. We are being changed from glory to glory (2 Cor. 3:18). Fathers put a badge on their family members, including themselves, which reads, "Please be patient with me. God isn't finished with me yet!"

Fathers develop fathers. A man learns how to father from a father. A father grows in fatherhood by leaning on the Father.

The goal of fathering is to develop men who can father and women who can mother under the covering of a godly husband. So when your son starts to make decisions as good as or better than you have been making, you can then loose the father in him. Jesus promised us that when we are in the Father and the Father is in us just as the Father is in Him, then we will do greater works than Christ did (John 14:12).

In other words, if your child is only as good as you, you have failed as a father. If your child is less then you, you have failed.

A successful father will produce a child who is greater than himself.

In conclusion, we now turn to a final issue facing our societies on fathering the fatherless.

Principles

- The godly father who develops his family has a plan for their orderly growth—physically, intellectually, emotionally, and spiritually.

- Development creates an environment that is conducive to others encountering learning experiences under the guidance of a father's wisdom.

- The objective of development is permanent growth. Therefore, a godly father provides encouragement, positive feedback, an opportunity to try and fail, and does not make comparisons.

- Fathers develop fathers. A man learns how to father from a father. A father grows in fatherhood by leaning on the Father.

- A godly father is an example of holiness for his family and develops them to be the light of the world, salt of the earth, and witnesses for Christ in the world.

- As developers, fathers plan, prepare, plant, protect, and produce that which God has placed in their care.

- A husband and father stretches his wife and children to achieve their utmost for His highest. He cultivates his relationship with his family so that they can be grow beyond themselves and be the saints God purposed them to be.

CONCLUSION

FATHERING THE FATHERLESS

I pray that godly fathers who read this book will receive the spirit of the Father—not just for their own families, but also for the church and our culture.

The spirit of a father is the awareness that everyone around a father is a father's responsibility.

Woman and children came out of the male man as we have studied in Genesis 1 & 2. So every woman and child that a father meets is his responsibility if they are fatherless. All the children in the world came out of a man, so we must father any of them that are fatherless.

Godly fathers must become fathers of their communities and nations.

We must realize that all of the children of society are our responsibility. There are many women and children who have a "daddy" but no "father". So we, as Christian fathers, must be sure that we take responsibility for those who are fatherless. James writes, *"Religion that*

God *our Father accepts as pure and faultless is this: to look after orphans and widows in their distress and to keep oneself from being polluted by the world.*" (James 1:27).

The fatherless should be fathered by Christian fathers.

There's a fathering parable in Matthew 25 in which Jesus reveals that those who truly follow Him—the Everlasting Father—will father those who are in prison, hungry, naked, thirsty, sick, and a stranger. Men, inasmuch as we father the least of these, we minister unto the Lord Himself. David declared, "*A father to the fatherless, a defender of widows, is God in his holy dwelling. God sets the lonely in families . . .*" (Ps. 68:5).

What is the family into which God places the fatherless? It is His family, the church. We are to go to wherever the fatherless are found and become a father and family to them.

Many of those in prison are men who never had a father like the Father. How do we heal that? Godly fathers must go out and father them. Recall once more the prophecy for our day in Malachi 4:6: "*And he shall turn the heart of the fathers to the children, and the heart of the children to their fathers, lest I [God] come and smite the earth with a curse.*" When godly fathers fail to father the fatherless in a society, a curse comes upon that land. Scripture never mentions returning the hearts of the children back to the mothers because we don't have a mother problem; we have a father problem.

*We must incorporate the scriptural functions
of fatherhood into our lives so that we will
finally understand and fulfill our true
priority, position, and role as a male.*

God the Father is our source. Masses of men must return to God the Father so that their children's hearts may be turned to their fathers and to God. We need men of the Spirit to be responsible as progenitors and providers for the future generations, and men who are fathers to be willing to sustain their offspring.

As a father—like *the* Father—remember that every child you meet is your child. You have a responsibility to support and pray for their godly father or to be a godly father for those who are fatherless. Every woman you meet is your baby. Every woman needs to be treated with dignity and respect.

This book is a clarion call to men to be the fathers God the Father created them to be. It is time that godly fathers answer God's call to be responsible for the fatherless in their churches, communities, and nations.

In Africa, there is a well-known concept: It takes a village to raise a child. That concept is also found in the Bible as it relates to embodying a corporate personality. The whole nation is responsible for each person, and the destiny of each person is shaped by the whole people. We have a corporate responsibility to father our fatherless. We are not in this alone. Together, we are a community of faith in the church that is God's family in which every member supports and cares for every other member.

I believe that the church should form the most magnificent and magnanimous adoption agency in the twenty-first century. The way you change a nation is not by attacking the government, but by fathering children and the fatherless. That's the way God did it in every situation. Therefore, godly fatherhood is the key to this generation and all to come.

Consider this final thought: God's Son entered into this world and had to be adopted by an earthly father—Joseph. Joseph could have rejected Mary as an unwed, unfaithful mother, but he didn't. At great personal risk and sacrifice to himself, Joseph stepped out responsibly and fathered Jesus, Savior of the world; yet, we never hear Jesus quote Joseph. Why? Because Joseph was a great father. Joseph must have done a great job fathering Jesus because you never hear Jesus quoting Joseph, only the Father. Joseph taught Jesus the ways of the Father and became a stellar model of fatherhood for all time!

Fathers, be like The Father to your own family, communities, and nations. Turn the heart of the children back to the father, and future generations will rise up and give glory to the Father.

Principles

- The spirit of a father is the awareness that everyone around a father is a father's responsibility.

- Godly fathers become fathers of their communities and nations.

- As Christian fathers, we are to go to wherever the fatherless are found and become a father and family to them.

- When we incorporate the fatherhood functions in our lives, we will finally understand our true priority, position, and roles as males.

- By being a father like the Father to your family, community, and nation, you are turning the hearts of the children back to the father, and future generations will rise up and give glory to the Father.

Other Titles by Myles Munroe

Becoming a Leader (Book, Workbook, and Video)
Seasons of Change
Myles Munroe on Leadership
Marriage 101
Sex 101
Singles 101
Single, Married, Separated & Life After Divorce (Book and Video)
Understanding Your Potential (Book and Video)
Releasing Your Potential (Book and Video)
Maximizing Your Potential (Book and Video)
In Pursuit of Purpose (Book and Video)
The Ministers Topical Bible
The African Cultural Heritage Topical Bible
Video - The Church
Video - The Hidden Glory
Video - The Kingdom of Ignorant Kings
Video - Maximizing Your Singleness
Video - The Golden Keys to Fulfilling Your Vision